A Quick Referen

Buying

A Small Business

in the UK

*A Fast Track to Understanding the Process of Buying a
Small to Medium Sized Business (under £20M)*

Ken Gorman

Table of Contents

Preface

This book is dedicated to all those brave souls who feel their calling is to buy a business but have never made it all the way through the process. I wrote this book as I saw so many good people spend months and years trying to fulfil this dream only to see failure after failure after months of hard work, often just on the brink of closing their first deal. This part is understandable...the merger and acquisitions game is hard, very hard. And beyond that, there are many misconceptions and false expectations about what it takes to get the right deal over the line.

This book is designed to be a starting point for new Buyers to at least have a foundational understanding of the process and many challenges they may encounter. The book is meant to be used as a companion guide while working with Transworld M&A and letting us manage your first transaction. The book is not meant to be read and implemented as a DIY project for a new Buyer or replace comprehensive new business buyer training programs (i.e. the Business Buyers Club in the UK). There are still 100's of twists and turns that could not be covered in any book or course and we believe we can add tremendous value in getting your first deal over the line.

There are three main benefits of working with us and letting us manage the transaction from beginning to end using our Dynamic M&A Transaction Management Program (DTM):

- The chance the transaction closes will be greatly increased
- The time it takes to close the transaction will be greatly reduced

- The Buyer and Seller will be on a good footing for a good post-sale relationship

One of the commonly understood statistics is that somewhere around 75% of small business transactions do not make it from Heads of Terms (where the Buyer and Seller agree on the commercials) to the closing table. Following that, 50% of the deals that do close don't deliver the value expected 2 years on which can mean everything from not exceeding expectations to liquidation. <u>The cost of these failures in terms of time and money can be significant for the Buyer.</u>

Another misconception is that once a Seller is found, a transaction can be completed in a short time scale like a month or two. For people who are inexperienced, this is wishful thinking...there are so many moving parts to the process and just the legal side can drag on for months if not properly managed. To put the cost of this delay in context, if you are buying a business with say £520K in after-tax profit...<u>this would mean that every week a transaction is delayed costs you £10K in lost income!</u> Many people don't understand this and try to cut costs by not getting good advisors and the right systems, only to have this turned upside down with delays running into months.

However, buying a small business can also be very rewarding when it works. There is no better (legal) return on investment when the model is working. Also, owning a business gives a new Buyer a channel for expression and a vehicle for serving the community...as well as building wealth for them and their family. So in most cases, it is well worth the effort and both Buyer and Seller win

I have spent over 10,000 hours running transactions and closed over 50 deals and been involved with over 100. Or, the way it feels is 10,000 hours of mistakes and learning from those mistakes. So I know deals can be closed and we can run a process that is successful most of the time. Although challenges can often seem infinite, most of the dozens of issues that arise during the process do repeat themselves in some form and have had solutions previously, so experience matters.

Transworld M&A is over 40 years old with 250+ offices globally (15 in the UK) and we sell over $1.5B worth of business annually. Being a Transworld M&A advisor requires extensive training and often advisors have advanced certifications and years of business experience. But most of all, a successful advisor has learned from 1000s of hours of field experience through both successes and failures and used our proven Dynamic Transaction Management Program to make sure everything stays on time and transitions close as quickly as possible.

The details of how to buy a business and the school of hard knocks are not something someone buying a business once every few years should have to go through...there is help! We can use our experience to make your business buying experience easier, faster and have a much greater chance of getting over the line. This book is about providing a reasonable foundation to engage with us in the process, not to encourage you to learn whatever is not in the book the hard way...save that for the lessons your new business will teach you!

So, we hope you get value from the book and please let us know when you are ready to engage your first business sale project and we will be happy to help. Please feel free to contact me and my team if you have an acquisition you need help with.

Ken Gorman

Managing Director Transworld M&A UK LSW

KGorman@transworldukmanda.com

Chapter 1 - 10 Great Reasons to Buy a Business

There are many great reasons to buy a business and in fact, you should expect it is one of the most exciting, life-changing things that you ever do! Next to getting married and having children, the act of buying or selling a business can be the biggest life event for many people. It is to this that we dedicate our work as M&A Advisors, to helping people embark on this very important life transaction.

I personally consider it a privilege to work with the business Buyers and Sellers that have been my clients and my vocation to make sure they get the right transaction for them, in a timely manner and that they have a chance of sleeping at night during the process. We thought we would start this book off in a positive way with a list of 10 good reasons to buy a business, although there are probably many more:

1. Freedom - Running your own business gives most people freedom. Freedom to express themselves, freedom to serve the community in their way, freedom from supervisors and being fired, freedom of creativity, time freedom and hopefully, financial freedom. In most cases, there is also the freedom of when to work and where to work. Of course, this is all subject to the demands of the customers and the operational demands of the business.

One of the goals of most entrepreneurs is to move in the direction of operator to owner to investor. At each stage the Seller is needed less and less in the business and with each stage comes more freedom. It also makes the business easier to sell as the Seller is not integral to the operations and so does not create a key person issue. This can take years to accomplish, but with diligent effort and understanding that this level of freedom is one of the objectives of the business, it can be achieved in most cases (often with the help of a business scaling coach).

There is one caveat to the pursuit of freedom for its own sake. We have seen some new business owners be so successful that they feel they have lost their freedom *to HR issues, VAT reports, legal issues, doing everything for 60 hours+ a week, etc. and come to us and feel the solution is to sell their business to get their freedom back. We always counsel that generally there is a better way than selling as a successful business producing yearly cash flow is a great thing to have and hard to replicate. The solution often is simply to change the way of working to get their freedom back, although this is very difficult to do without help. Fortunately, help is at hand. There are great business scaling coaches that can help with structuring your business to delegate more and get your freedom back while still enjoying the fruits of your business. One of them has written a guest chapter later in this book.*

2. Financial Return - Making a Good Living - It goes without saying that if you own a business, you control the bank account and can pay yourself what you want within the limits of the profits, business plan and good tax advice. This is different from having a salary that you have, a 3rd party owner or a boss that you need to negotiate with every year. If the business does well, this allows you to extract a good living. For some of our clients, a very good 7-figure living!

How you pay yourself is a matter for you and your tax advisor. Usually, a minimal amount is PAYE and dividends make up quite a big portion, but these can be paid to family members who have a small shareholder to minimise tax. So there are many opportunities to not only make a good living but to minimise tax which are not available if you are an employee of someone else's company.

3. Financial Return - Building Wealth - As the business and profits grow, so does the value of the business if you decide to sell. So not only are you receiving the profits in a given year, but the level of profit is simultaneously increasing the value of the business so a sort of double bubble.

From an investment perspective, the leverage factor is staggering if the business does well based on a small investment from the Buyer.

Let's run through an example:

> **Enterprise Value -** Your target company has EBITDA of £600K (and after-tax income of £500K), in this example you decide to purchase this company for £1.8M (3x).
>
> **Offer -** You offer the Seller a closing payment of £1M which comprises £300K of your money (your total investment is £400K as you need to cover £100K in acquisition costs) and £700K from a bank cash flow loan over 5 years plus £800K deferred payments to the Seller (£1.8M - £1M) over 4 years or £200K per year.
>
> **Debt -** This means total debt payments are £200K for the deferred and about £200K for the bank loan leaving you £100K excess each year.
>
> **Growth -** Over the 5 years you increase the EBITDA by 10% a year so at the end of 5 years, EBITDA is up to £1M.
>
> **Exit -** After 5 years, all the loans are paid off and you sell the business for a 4x multiple (as EBITDA is higher) * £1M in EBITDA or £5M in sale value.
>
> **Return of Investment -** Your return on your £400K investment is a staggering 1250 %! (12x+).

Profit Along the Way - Additionally, you have collected the extra profit along the way which you may have put into a SASS pension, further reducing tax and building wealth (another conversation with your wealth manager).

This is a somewhat simplistic example, but it makes the point of how leveraged owning a business is when it goes according to plan.

4. Community Impact - Many people care deeply about making an impact in the community. For many, this is as important as making money and brings them even more joy. By definition, most businesses are supplying some service that the community needs to function or bring more ease and happiness to the people in the community.

Doing a good job with your product or service makes people's lives easier and contributes to the well-being of the community. In fact, when we step out of our homes, almost all the services we are using beyond the government supplied services and those nature provides fall into this category. So owning a business that does a good job at a reasonable price is a tremendous way to be of service to the community.

5. Family Legacy - Many people don't just want to earn money for themselves but want other family members to benefit as well as be able to leave wealth for future generations. A business is a multi-dimensional vehicle for achieving just this. While you are in the business, the wealth being generated can be used to benefit the whole family. Family members can come into the business to learn certain skills, get their first jobs or just earn pocket money.

A business is a great vehicle to sponsor programs and events that other family members may be involved in. You may also be able to help family members abroad who want to come to the UK with things like work permits. So there are many possibilities to benefit the family while you own the business.

Retirement planning and wealth transfer to children is also very multifaceted. Shares can be transferred at low tax rates and many inheritance taxes don't apply. Family SASS pensions are also a great way to invest profits from the business with all the family members in one program. Please speak with your wealth manager who will specialise in this area.

6. Personal Growth - Running a business can be one of life's great challenges. Small businesses are very much a function of the growth of the owner in being able to expand their own thinking and navigate the business through a changing business landscape and also growth. Many business owners seek out coaching programs to help them grow personally and constantly develop ever better, more effective business strategies and personal strategies...something they might never do just as an employee.

There is no shortage of challenges from financial, staff motivation, leadership, customers, and products...and finding personal balance in the middle of all of it can be daunting. This process can also be very rewarding as challenges are overcome and real change happens...or debilitating if the person is not really made for this kind of experience. The type of person that thrives on these challenges we call an X-Factor leader which is covered in a later chapter.

7. Being Part of the Business Community - There are some amazing people running businesses in the community who have a unique perspective that someone that is an employee would not necessarily have. These people often belong to specialised networking, political and social groups. Being a business owner often qualifies you to be part of these groups in a way that might not otherwise be possible.

8. Starting a Business From Scratch is Much Harder - The general statistic that is discussed is that only 20% of businesses are even still trading after 5 years and only 10% after 10 years. Of the ones that are still trading, the vast majority never make it over £1M in turnover.

People often point to the IT sector, which is largely funded by Venture Capital (VC). In the VC model, they will invest in something like 5 companies expecting 3 to not make it, one to break even and one to be the star that pays for the rest...not great odds if you are betting on your family's future!

It is very difficult to start from scratch, figure out customer demand, build the systems and hire the right people...to get the formula just right so to speak. Once a business gets the formula right after 1000s of tweaks and the right team, it often takes off and is very scalable. So in buying a business, you are buying a proven formula...if the business has been around more the 5 years the chances it will survive another 5 are very high...and 10 years even better.

9. A Creative Outlet - Many people want a creative outlet for their efforts in life, sort of a life's work so to speak. The right kind of business can offer this while simultaneously being of great service to the community. Owning a business gives you the opportunity to try things and see what works. In fact, this process is essential for success. There are endless challenges to overcome that test creativity and ingenuity.

The best business owners we encounter are very proud of their companies. From the service they deliver that has been perfect through many years of improvements, to their branding and websites, their culture, their investment strategies, etc. A successful business is often the result of a prolonged creative process by the owner and those close to him/her that has tangible results that can be very rewarding.

10. Having Fun! - When you add all of these up, for many people running a business is just fun. It can also be a lot of hard work, but often the activities that are the most fun in life are like that. But it should be fun and rewarding. Knowing this from the onset will cause a new buyer to veer towards businesses they will enjoy running. We think it is a fallacy that enjoying the business you run has to be sacrificed for maximum financial gain. Our experience is that one drives the other. The most successful businesses we encounter tend to be with owners who really enjoy running those businesses.

We also wanted to mention that even though a certain business may not have an exciting product or be considered to be in a 'fun' sector, it can still be fun to run. The ability to execute well, build a rewarding culture, have satisfied customers, watch people grow, make money, etc. can be fun in itself!

Chapter 2 - What is The Right Business to Buy?

What really matters is what is the best business for you, the individual Buyer. As everyone is different with different backgrounds, skills and desires, this is specific for each individual Buyer. So it is worth considering who you are and what type of situation would work for you.

Notice that we are not going straight to some kind of discussion on verticals, financials or growth sectors (although they are very important and we will get there later) as we believe that 'cultural fit' and the nature of the people really make transactions successful so this needs to be discussed/understood in the first instance.

We estimate over 90% of people that try to buy a business never will successfully close for many reasons. Of those that do, over half will struggle to run it successfully. So who are the Buyers that are in the 10% that will be successful? This is an important question as getting it right can save an enormous amount of time and money.

Firstly, it is worth considering why the person who owns and built the business you are trying to Buy has been successful. We believe much of this success can often be summed up in a blanket term we call **X-Factor Leadership**. This differs from management, which involves the day-to-day running of the business. This is actually the aspect that has guided and provided inspiration for the business to get where it is today. An X-Factor leader also navigated the business through the ups and downs that are inevitable in running any business over a number of years to the point where it is profitable and sellable as an ongoing concern today.

We mention 'leadership' specifically, as generally there are very good 'managers' in the business but leadership is a different concept. A manager is a different type of person that is excellent at their day-to-day job but they are generally working under an X-Factor Leader that has provided the context for their role. Most often, X-Factor type leaders will not work under other X-Factor leaders (not for very long anyway) so the fact managers have been in place for a significant period often demonstrates they are not this type of personality.

Often, the current managers could be mentored into X-Factor leadership type people, but this would require a process and people from outside the company over a period of time and for the right type of person. It is not just something that just automatically happens any more than someone becoming a star football striker just because they have played on the team for a few years when the star striker leaves.

As an example, during the Covid period, a manager who was well trained in how to run the business in a certain way might have come to a standstill when the regular customer activity dried up. However, X-Factor leaders were often able to completely pivot their company to survive or even take advantage of the situation the pandemic caused. Many did this effortlessly and came out the other side stronger.

Many businesses that did not have an X-Factor leader continued operating and managing as they were and slowly shrunk out of existence. This debunks the idea a good 'management team' alone can somehow drive and grow a business long-term just by doing the same things. It takes an X-Factor leader to drive constant change, adaptation and growth.

However, in a business sale, very often this X-Factor leader is leaving (as generally, their leaving is the purpose of a business sale in the first place). But who is going to fill the 'leadership void' that is created? Is it one of the current management team?

Very often managers are not X-Factor leaders, they only work for them. Usually, an X-Factor leader will not work for another X-Factor leader for long, they will leave to start their own project. So when you have good managers that have been in place for a long time, generally they are just that...good managers.

In our observation, the important point is simply to recognise that this potential 'leadership void' (versus management) that may occur when the Seller leaves exists and needs to be addressed as an integral part of the deal structure. And also to avoid the pitfall of thinking that the day-to-day operating managers will be able to 'lead' the business without this leadership void being addressed in some way.

But this void must be filled somehow and often this is the catalyst of why they want to sell the business. Their time has come to leave and they need someone else to come in and continue and grow their legacy. So very often this is one of the main criteria for being a good Buyer is being able to fill the leadership void with one or more strategies.

Filling the X - Factor Leadership Void

There are several ways in which we have observed this leadership void being addressed that can work (in fact being in denial that this is an issue is the biggest problem in our experience).

The Private Equity Approach - Private Equity companies generally 'do not run businesses, or so they say. The Private Equity firms are very good at identifying existing management team members who have potential and then surrounding them with an experienced, generally non-exec, leadership team. This will typically mean a chairman who is from the industry, a CFO and other advisors on the board who can support the specific type of business.

Starting during due diligence, they meticulously work with the new CFO and management team to develop 5 year plans with specific metrics they will use for managing the business. The management team that takes this journey will typically be incentivised with significant Sweet Equity shares that will often allow them to retire should the business hit the 5 year goals they have set out. In our experience, the Private Equity directors are still very involved after the sale at a Board Level to support and guide the business.

Trade Buyers - A trade Buyer has the advantage of often understanding the Seller's business and in fact, they may be a direct competitor. They may simply be able to leverage their existing leadership team (which is probably headed up by an X-Factor Leader). Very often, they can cross-pollinate management over to the business they are buying. Sometimes they will simply be buying customers or staff and the business does not need to keep running in the current form.

Operator Buyers - An operator Buyer is most often an X-Factor Leader in their own right with previous industry experience and track record running a business generally related to the sector they are looking at. They may already understand and have run a business similar to the one they are considering buying. Occasionally, they will be buying a business in a new sector and can make an agreement with the new owner to mentor them for an extended period (like 1 year +).

But the one commonality is that the Operator Buyer understands that they need to be actively involved in the 'leadership' (versus day-to-day management) of the company. For example, they will need to spend a year to 18 months actively involved in running the business to understand it and maintain a board level leadership role afterwards.

Team Member - In this model, the individual recognises that they are not an X-Factor leader and will need to be on a team with someone who is. They may have finance skills, for example, and be a team member with another X-Factor leader who is going to take the role of filling the leadership void.

Investor Buyer - Our observation is that the idea someone can just buy a business they don't have a background and are unwilling to become an operator with the idea of just relying on the existing day-to-day managers does not work well in most cases and a flawed model. If someone is not an X-Factor leader and/or not prepared to fill the leadership void, they will need to be on a team or investing in someone that is to lead the business post-sale. We realise that many people in the community and some Buyer programs may advocate for this 'investor only' model. We are simply being true to our observations that this does not work in practice in most cases.

It is important to understand that the due diligence period and contracts phase could take 3-6 months. During this time a Seller is going to get to know a Buyer pretty well. They will need to be confident that a Buyer can take over and run their business or they are likely to pull out of the deal. In the first instance, they will want confidence that their legacy will be maintained. In the second, they will want to be confident that they will get paid any monies due after closing. So it makes sense, to be honest about whether a Buyer is the right fit early on to save both sides time and money.

What Type of Business Should I Buy?

This is a multidimensional question that is different for everyone. This topic is also covered in many other books, so we won't go into it much here. However, below are some thoughts and guidelines you might find helpful:

A Sector That You Understand - Warren Buffett is famous for saying that he would not buy a business he doesn't understand. We agree and in fact, believe that if you are going to fill the X-Factor leader role you really need to have some kind of background in the sector you are buying into or be prepared for an extended mentoring process by the existing owner (maybe years).

A Sector That You Like - This goes with the previous point, if you like a sector you are going to want to learn more about it, leading to understanding that sector well. Also, this ties into every point on why to buy a business...if you are inspired by a sector you are likely to be more creative, offer a better service to the community, work harder, be more committed, want to get people involved, etc...all of these generally lead to good financial results.

A Company That Inspires You - Liking the sector is important, but to be truly successful you will probably need vision. To have vision you need to be inspired by the market you are surviving and whatever it is you are offering them. This inspiration is infectious and can turn the business into more than just a job for the employees with significant productivity and service level results.

Geography Matters - You are going to need to spend time at the business, with the people and with the customers, at the very least. Although much of business can be done remotely, there is no substitute for meeting people and there are generally many people beyond just employees and customers that benefit from face time. Due to this, being close enough to attend the area where these people are is very important. The idea you can buy a business and be 200 miles away from most of the people and not cause a massive headache is unrealistic in most cases.

A Business You Can Afford - As will be discussed in the chapters on valuation and deal structuring, there is a certain amount of your own capital that will be needed for costs and also a closing payment in most cases. You want to make sure the amount you have to put in mirrors the business you are looking at and that you do not overstretch yourself. The idea you can just get as much debt as you want is generally not accurate. For one thing, the banks won't just lend with significant scrutiny. Also, the cash flow has to be sufficient to pay the debt back. So it is prudent to understand what Enterprise Value range and terms are going to work for you.

Recurring/Repeating Revenue - The value of recurring/repeat revenue is talked about a lot and is, of course, true. In the end, you are buying a future cash flow and the less risk there is around this actually coming in, the better. Sometimes repeating revenue is the best kind to have as the customers will just keep their contracts running indefinitely as long as there is no friction. This can even be better than long-term contracts, which may have an endpoint or a 'cliff'. But in both cases, the customers are baked in and the business does not need to find new customers for the bulk of the revenue which lowers risk.

However, this is a general concept that must be evaluated in detail for all types of businesses on a case-by-case basis. There are many nuances and some businesses that rely on a new customer or new contracts on a regular basis are great businesses.

Room for Lots of Growth - In theory, the leverage buy-out model can work ok with flat revenue (when the debt is paid in 5 years and the business can be sold again for the same price, mathematically the return is still very good for the original investment). However, it is commonly understood that businesses are either growing are dying so this is not a great strategy.

Also, business is in a constant state of flux with the loss of some customers and markets and others added, so a business owner generally wants somewhere to grow into. One of the main features of buying a small business is to be able to improve and scale the model, so there needs to be a market to scale into. Growth is exciting and just a small amount of growth each year, like 10%, can double the ROI over 5 years.

Be Careful of Capital Equipment Refresh - Businesses that are capital intensive need to have this capital equipment refreshed on a regular basis. Often when a sale comes up, the owners have put this off and been 'sweating' the assets. This leaves a new buyer needing to use cash to implement a refresh program. If this was not understood at the time of purchase, it can cause a lot of problems. If this is understood, it can be managed and modelled and is usually not a problem.

Good Systems - Most businesses are about the people that deliver the service which is true. But these people need to be organised through good systems. The people should have figured out 1000s of details about how to optimise their service to the customer and this should be understood, repeatable and documented so new people can be trained and KPIs monitored.

When you are buying a business, a big part of what you are buying is these systems. If they are not well documented and sloppy, when the owner leaves, it could cause serious disruption to the operations of the company. A company with good, well-documented systems is much easier to take over and absorb the loss of any staff.

This goes hand in hand with good books and records. Understanding business performance metrics is critical to managing any business (if you can't measure it, you can't manage it is the old axiom). Poor books and records cast doubt on whether the business results are accurate at all and whether the products and services being delivered are profitable. Not understanding that can lead to the wrong decisions and weaknesses in managing cash flow, which is one of the leading causes of businesses going out of business.

People You Like - The leading cause of business sales not getting to the closing table or not delivering after the sale, even if it does can usually be traced back to what we call 'poor cultural fit'. We use the term 'cultural fit' as it encompasses people with similar values, a similar vibe, and people that like each other and are able to formulate a common objective and have fun with it. We find that almost always the deals that make it to the closing table are when the Buyer and Seller take an instant liking to each other in the first meeting. In fact, this is one of the main things we look for early on, call it chemistry.

You might wonder why this matters if the owner is leaving? The reason is that the owner generally reflects the culture of the company as a whole. This is not always the case and sometimes it is the number 2 person that is staying in the business if the owner has been out of the business for a significant period but then the same goes for the chemistry with this number 2 person. At some point, a Buyer should feel that he really likes these people and is looking forward to working with them and vice versa. These are the transactions that survive the rest of the process and delivery after closing as a general rule.

Chapter 3 -

The Seven Deadly Sins When Buying a Business - By Jeff Lermer, Chartered Accountant

---

I very much appreciate being asked to prepare this guest chapter in a very important publication, because this publication is the beginning of your journey to buying a business. As a Chartered Accountancy Practice, we help businesses in many ways and I'm gonna look at a number of sections as I have described as the seven deadly sins of buying a business.

The seven deadly sins are as follows:

1. Not defining what you are buying
2. Using the wrong entity for buying a business
3. Not doing proper due diligence
4. Not knowing the value / agreeing on the price – paying for potential, understanding goodwill
5. Not budgeting cash flow, or understanding what you are buying
6. Not knowing what you don't know
7. Not understanding tax

1. Not Defining What You Are Buying

You may have an idea of what you're buying, and the target may have an idea of what they are selling, but as you can imagine, too young and inexperienced lovers (apologies for the terrible analogy), trying to model something without actually knowing what they are doing is a recipe for disaster.

There are a number of areas of misunderstanding, are you buying the shares in the company or are you just buying the assets? Are you buying some of the assets or all of them and are you taking on the liabilities? If you are buying the shares, what will be left on the balance sheet and how much would be taken out? How much of the Target company to treat as a distribution prior to the sale?

In order to avoid these problems, you need to be completely clear about what you are buying. If you are buying the asset, and if you find a company you need to define exactly what the balance sheet would look like post sale. As an accountant, I like numbers, and it is clear to me if you have defined exactly what you were buying. Many vendors believe the cash in the company is theirs, while the acquirer might think that money will be used to finance the business going forward. These are genuine misunderstandings that need to be sorted out.

2. Using The Wrong Entity For Buying A Business

You must first decide if you are buying the assets or the shares. Also, if you are buying the assets personally or in a limited company as the taxes are very different. If there are deferred payments, how does this work and what are the specific guarantees being given?

I am normally a fan of acquiring assets, not shares. If you acquire the shares, you also acquire potential liabilities that are within that company. For example, if the previous owner has made mistakes on VAT, or PAYE, or has disagreements with the amount of what they are owed or owe, you take on all those obligations.

Yes, it is true that you can cover these with tax warranties, but it's far easier to avoid this with an asset sale. The majority of very small acquisitions are carried out as asset sales in the transactions that we work on because they are simpler and cheaper.

Notwithstanding this, the reason that share sales are popular is the tax treatment from the vendor's point of view. In a simple way, they simply exit the business. The vendors agree on a price for the shares. They resign and you take over removing what is agreed.

The normal process, if you are buying the shares or all the assets, is that you use a special-purpose vehicle and potentially a holding company. A special-purpose vehicle (SPV) is just a new company formed for acquiring the assets and liabilities on the sale, all the shares in a share sale.

The reason I will advocate using an SPV is to manage the risk if all goes wrong. The liabilities for the acquisition will be held in the SPV and if you have bought a complete disaster, and unfortunately that is more common than you might think, you can limit your liability via the company.

I'm sure if you have reviewed the chapters in this book, the term deferred consideration is mentioned. That is a position where you pay for the assets, or the shares, over a period of time in the future. The term vendor finance is also used. This is particularly common and useful, especially when you cannot agree on the share price.

I will give you one very true life example:

Typically, in the construction industry, small construction companies are worth, in my opinion, very little. The vendor believes there will be a whole stream of work coming to that company, but contractually all the acquirer gets is the contract that is signed on the date of the sale. There is a massive gap in expectations and to breach that gap you might agree to some sort of deferred consideration that is contingent on future activity. This may be a percentage of turnover or a percentage of profits. I'm probably a fan of a percentage of turnover on the basis that this number is significantly easier to calculate and agree on, while profit is extremely subjective.

Above the SPV, you may decide to use a holding company. The benefit of a holding company is really if you plan to acquire more than one business, and you wish to separate these businesses.

Please see the diagram below:

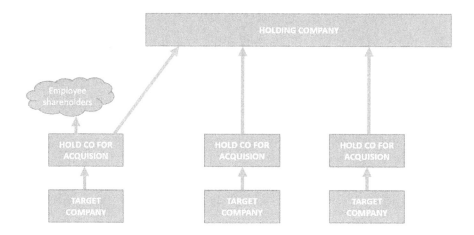

You will also see a little bubble on the left-hand side of the diagram which says employee shareholders. This is not essential, but it's sometimes useful to offer some shares to existing share in existing employees as they may be key to this acquisition being successful for you. Caution should be taken here, as your rights need to be protected, and you need the ability to buy back those shares at an agreed price at some stage in the future, but it may be a good way of bringing in loyalty, support, and the right help you need at this stage.

3. Not Doing Proper Due Diligence

Anyone considering acquiring a business needs to check all the assumptions that are being made in the deal.

Financial due diligence provides peace of mind to you by analysing and validating all the financial, commercial, operating and strategic assumptions that you have made in buying the business. In my opinion, it will give you significant and necessary confirmation. Just getting into the business, looking around, checking emails, reviewing information like the complaints log, and chatting to the team about what's going on will give you a really good feel for the business. Also, looking at the numbers, the VAT returns, and any mistakes made will indicate how well the business is run.

If you are not buying the business, it may seem like you are looking a gift horse in the mouth, but it may not be such a gift. I'm not a fan of using Latin, but the phrase caveat emptor is completely relevant here, which means Buyer, beware. It is up to you to check what you are buying. The themes to look at our as follows:

> Administration
> Financial
> Human resources
> Assets
> Taxes
> Intellectual property
> Legal matters
> Customers

4. Not Knowing The Value / Agreeing The Price – Paying For Potential, Understanding Goodwill

The fourth big mistake, people make is not knowing or agreeing the value of what they are buying, and paying for potential and not understanding what goodwill is.

This may seem to seem obvious, but how do we know if the business we are being offered is being offered to us at the right price? The correct price is what you were prepared to pay and what the Seller is prepared to receive, based on the full information.

The goodwill would be defined as the difference between the assets and the future profits that will be generated from the assets.

How much would you pay now for the expectation of these profits? There should be a maximum price, although other items matter too, especially with no money down.

The value today of any business, in theory anyway, is the discounted sum of the future cash flows being generated. But a big mistake is paying for the potential that you are adding.

It's very easy to run away and to overvalue potential. Even if you're putting little or no money down, you don't want to just buy a job; you want to buy a business that will grow, thrive and give you a return at the end. Especially if you're investing in fashionable technologies, you may get overexcited about the potential, ignoring the hard work that you will have to do to make that potential happen.

A great client of mine once described an ideal business to buy and I completely agree with his summary. He said if it's a sort of business where you are sitting at a dinner party boasting about, feeling amazing about, thinking you rule the world because it's so up-to-date and fashionable yet it's probably a business that is not making much money. The businesses that really succeed are the ones nobody really talks about, the ones that just produce a good sustainable growing profit each year in an unexciting market. I think this advice is liquid gold.

Goodwill does exist and this may be based on things like the value of a company's brand name, its solid customer base, its good customer relations, good employee relations, and proprietary technology which allows it to make more profits than its competitors, or provide things that these competitors cannot provide.

5. Not Bothering With Looking At The Budget And Future Cash Flow, Or Understanding What You Are Buying

It's important to produce a cash, flow analysis, and budget, including factoring in tax, and the management time that you will need to put into the business. If you do not produce a budget, how are you going to know you are going to make a profit from this business? Relying on vendor assurances is something you must never do. I cannot emphasise how important it is to produce a budget prior to acquiring the business, so you know you could afford to run it, pay the vendors if there is deferred consideration, pay the tax, pay the employees, replace machinery that needs to be replaced, etc.

And it's a harsh reality to say, but if the budget says no, you just say No!

6. Not Knowing What You Do Not Know

There are a number of things to consider here, and these are as follows:

Working with people like Ken Gorman at Transworld M&A, and using the skills that they have because buying a business is not necessarily just intuitive, there are lots of tricks, shortcuts, pitfalls to avoid, and he knows what items to look for. Having someone experienced at your side makes all the difference.

There may be specific terms that are used in a transaction. You just don't understand them because you've not come across them in normal life. For example, the word whitewash may mean a number of things. I'm choosing this to mean an acquisition using the assets of the target Company in order to acquire the shares from the vendor via a loan to the SPV.

Financing and personal guarantees are something you should take specific advice on and use experts. It is possible to search the Internet and find these things but working with your "power team" and having good inroads into raising finance, and even producing something called personal guarantee insurance may be really useful for this acquisition.

You also may not have considered your future exit, structuring now can make a massive difference.

7. Not Understanding Tax

Tax can be looked at in many ways, but if you just treat it as a cost, it just becomes something that should be minimised. Just as an example of how simple structural changes make a huge example see the example below:

- Say Fred is buying Wilma Limited for £800k over 5 years that makes £250k per annum.

- **Without a holding company**, Fred buys the company personally and he has the obligation to pay the £160,000 pa. in deferred payments to the Seller.

- Wilma Limited makes £250,000 and pays say 25% tax so gives out a dividend to Fred of £187,500.

- The dividend is taxable and gives Fred a personal tax liability of £63,281 (or more!!, could be £737,781). so he has only £124,218 after tax yet still has to pay the £160K deferred to the Seller.

- **With a holding company,** Fred Limited buys Wilma LTD and he has the obligation to pay the £160,000 pa. deferred to the Seller as before.

- Wilma Limited makes £250,000, pays say 25% tax so gives out a dividend of £187,500 to Fred Limited.

- The dividend is not taxable in Fred Limited as no tax on dividends between UK companies, so Fred Limited has £187,500 to pay the £160,000 to the Seller.

Conclusion

I hope you have found this useful. The purpose of this chapter is to simply reflect on the importance of structure and planning when you acquire a business.

Chapter 4 - Who is The Business Seller?

The first thing to know is that most of these heroes have worked all hours and weathered the ups and downs of the business cycle to get to a point in their life where they can see the light at the end of the tunnel, a time when they can take a well-deserved break and think about retirement. And so begins the business exit process. We have found that working with the individuals that start, run and navigate the growth of successful companies are generally simply amazing people!

For most people selling a business is a HUGE life event. It can be as significant as getting married or having children and is often more emotionally complex. The process of selling a business most often arises due to a desire to retire, which is one of life's major transitions. Often a business is the most valuable asset a person owns and the sale will fund this retirement. So, in addition to the emotional side, selling their business may be the most important financial transaction of their lives.

Something like only 20% of companies make it to 5 years and 10% to 10 years and still are trading. For the ones that do make it, the vast majority never exceed £1M turnover. So our clients are normally in a very small, elite percentage of people that can buck the statistics and navigate companies through the ups and downs and over a long period of time to create successful companies that someone else would want to buy (the topic of this book).

These people deserve our respect. They have beat the odds to build a business that the community demonstrates is important by continuing to buy their products and services, taking care of their employees and generally providing a good living for the families. So these X-Factor leaders generally deserve our respect and admiration as a starting point for a relationship. In fact, being willing to consider buying someone's business for millions of pounds is in itself a great demonstration of respect, which is a great starting point.

Why Do Business Owners Sell?

The Retiree - In the small business space, generally the answer to this is...because it is time to leave. The best way to describe what we have observed is that there is a switch in the heart that goes off and says it's time to go. Sometimes, people are aware that this switch is coming and have a 3-5 year runway.

Often they have ignored this and now the switch is a very acute feeling and they feel life pulling them in another direction. Most often, this is due to retirement and a business sale not only becomes monetary but also buying time to do the things they want while they still have time.

Functional Exits - Another reason people want to sell their business is they have what we call a mechanical reason. For example, they are moving to another geography, they have a health issue that no longer allows them to run the business or a major life circumstance change. These are very straightforward situations and they just need to find a Buyer that can take over and get what they can monetarily.

The Young Overwhelmed Entrepreneur Syndrome - Sometimes you will get younger people with successful businesses that think they want to sell. Upon enquiry, what has happened is that they became an entrepreneur to get freedom (the most common motivation). Now that they have a successful business...there are staff issues, reporting requirements, legal issues and lots of problems to overcome and they find themselves doing everything. So their solution is often just to sell and take the money to get their freedom back.

The problem is that the majority of the time they will fall in love with the business during the sale process and realise how much money they could make (versus selling and being paid over a 3-5 year period) and pull out at the end leaving the Buyer with months of costs. Often the best approach with this type of business owner is to encourage them to engage a business scaling coach that will help them with delegation and company structuring to take the load off of them and get their freedom back that way.

The Serial Entrepreneur - There is another type we call the serial entrepreneur that builds businesses to a level and then genuinely tires of them and needs to move to the next one. Often, they are already running the next one. These are honest people that know where they sit in the business development cycle and these can often be great businesses. The trick is to distinguish this type of Buyer from the just overwhelmed Buyer above. Getting this wrong can result in months worth of work and a low chance of getting to the closing table.

What Do Business Owners Really Want

Most business owners have spent years working to become the best in their fields and have had many years of success as a result. When it comes time to leave their businesses, we have found that these same people had no idea how the process worked, how to maximise the value of their business, how long it would take and how to manage their own wealth as it related to their business to name a few.

Consequently, they only had a vague idea of the type of Buyer that would be ideal for their business and how the process would work. Often their ideas of what type of Buyer they wanted and why were misguided. To address this, we wrote an introductory book titled **'Selling Your Business - A Quick Reference Guide'**.

What we discovered is that most business owners really want the following:

Legacy Continuation - This is a blanket concept that means they want their business to be a better version of itself post-sale and all the people involved with the business to be taken care of. Many Sellers do not emphasize this initially when we meet them as they purport to be all about the money but we found in almost all cases 'legacy' turned out to be as or even more important than monetary considerations. Most business owners are successful because they have taken care of people and built loyal employees and customers, so this energy and inclination continues even during a business sale.

Legacy means their employees are taken care of, customers are served well, other relationship commitments are honoured, their brand increases in credibility (as it will always be attached to their name), etc. This means when we are running a sale process, addressing an area we call 'cultural fit' when it comes to Buyers and Sellers is critical. If people 'vibe' each other and the Buyer is a good fit for the business, this creates a scenario with the highest chance of the deal getting closed and a good result after the fact.

Money and Lower Risk - This is the obvious one as, of course, business owners want as much as they can get with the least risk. Part of this is about the money itself, as they may need it for retirement or something else. But often, our business Sellers are already wealthy, so the money becomes a testament to the value they have built. It is important to understand which of these is in play when deal creating structures.

Also, everyone wants less risk but there are many tradeoffs to risk and understanding the implications for each Buyer is critical. It should go without saying that no one likes the feeling of being 'ripped off' or selling something at a lower price than they think they should have got. It is embarrassing, it doesn't feel good. This is important to understand as a Buyer because a sale transaction can take many months and the Seller will have many people commenting (accountant, lawyer, friends, etc.) and if the deal feels unfair, this is likely to be discovered and the transaction may become a statistic when they pull out.

Physical Freedom - This ties into the first point about why people really sell. The switch in the heart that says it's time to go, time to do something different. Most often, the Sellers' new activities are already identified and often even underway. They need to sell the business so they can do that 3-month cruise, for example. It is important for a Buyer to understand these things as it can be helpful to remind the Seller of what they really want and the opportunities for these new activities if things get challenging during the sale process and/or they start having second thoughts.

Real Retirement - This is important and often misunderstood. This point refers to a mental state, not a physical one. Most business owners have lived with the pressures of their business on their shoulders and in their minds for most waking hours over the last many years and even decades. Real retirement is when the pressures of the business no longer live in their heads and they have genuine freedom. It is no use sitting on a beach in Spain if you spend half the time worrying about your business!

This needs to be understood as often Buyers position deal structures in purely financial terms, often not understanding why the owner does not want to roll some equity or has issues with lots of risk post-sale. Often the answer is that this scenario does not offer them 'real retirement' and another type of deal structure that may not look as financially advantageous may actually give them the peace of mind and freedom they are looking for (and deserve).

Chapter 5 - Timescales and Statistics

When asked "How long does it take to buy a business?" I frequently respond with the old adage, 'How long is a piece of string?'

This is not a particularly helpful answer, but it is at least an honest one. When new to the business buying process, I quickly learned that the financial data the Seller makes available provides some clues to a possible timescale but a multitude of other factors will impact the length of a particular business sale process.

Statistics for the Actual Business Sale Process

The first thing to understand is a few statistics to have a feel for how the business sale process actually pans out in reality:

8.2 Months - The International Business Brokers Association (IBBA) states that based on their research, the average business sells in 8.2 months. (It is important to note that these are averages so for larger, more complex businesses the time can actually be much longer).

75% Post Heads of Terms/Letter of Intent Drop Out Rate - The IBBA also reports that 75% of business sale transactions fall through 'after' offers are agreed upon between Buyer and Seller during the due diligence and contract phase. Yes, mathematically this means each Buyer on average will have three false starts (the fourth one wins) before getting to the end if they are even in the percentage of businesses that complete a successful transaction.

12% of Business Sell Who Go It Alone on Internet Sites - Another important statistic is that business owners who attempt to sell their business on their own through Internet sites are only successful about 12% of the time.

80%+ of Buyers Who Attempt to Buy Business Never End Up Buying One - There are many reasons for this which are covered throughout this book. As we have discussed, one of the main reasons is that the people attempting to buy a business are really not the right people to run businesses which results in multiple failure points during the process.

60% - 80% of Businesses That Go Up for Sell, Don't Sell - This is a statistic that is often quoted by business brokerage firms and probably has some truth to it. However, the statistic is skewed by High Street businesses (fast food, beauty etc.) that are often harder to sell. Also, often a Seller will put the business on the market and withdraw it if they can't get enough money or for personal reasons. But it makes the point...many businesses don't sell. For those good, profitable businesses with solid books and processes that do want to sell, the main reason they don't sell is a) lack of a sophisticated Buyer outreach program and b) lack of good process management during the due diligence/contract phase as above. (Fortunately, a good M&A Advisor can mitigate both of these issues).

Less than 50% of Businesses Sold Actually Deliver the Value Expected at the Time of Sale - This is a difficult statistic given how hard it is actually to get to a close. Upon further examination, the majority of the time this is caused by the failure to evaluate (and care about) a good cultural fit from the onset. Often business Buyers focus on spreadsheets, strategy and philosophy and forget they are buying a group of people that need to be integrated into another group of people and if this doesn't work many will leave and be less motivated...delivering a poor post-sale result.

Note: These are averages and are meant to give you a flavour of what the average business Buyer experiences. At Transworld M&A we have developed processes and expertise that significantly reduce timescales and increase the likelihood of getting to the closing table with the Buyers and Sellers having a good relationship and cultural fit. This is, in fact, the value add that we offer.

Business Sale Process Timescales

The 8.2 months previously quoted needs to be taken with a pinch of salt as this will include all businesses in the SME category, many of which could be quite small and the process happens more quickly. For comparison, let's examine a fish and chip shop on the high street alongside a complex manufacturing company with several sites, maybe some of them not even in the UK.

One would think that the fish and chips would sell faster than the complex machine shop. However, there is another factor which is that not all businesses even sell. If a business is not very sellable in the first place (i.e. it may have low profits or no profits) there is a long period during which the owner adjusts to the situation. It takes time to become accustomed to the fact that, if they want to sell their business at all, it will be for a very low price. This all adds elapsed time and influences the statistics, of course.

On the other hand, a complex machine shop with excellent books and records (see a later chapter on the importance of this), and great EBITDA, that is priced right with a highly motivated Seller can find a Buyer within 2 weeks of listing.

Yes, the due diligence and legal process will always take a few months longer than a fish and chip shop transaction but the deal will be completed in 6 months. The fish and chip business with poor books and records, overpriced with an owner who was not that motivated to sell will still be on the market. We could still be marketing this business

18 months later when the owner finally decides he really does want to sell and drops the price.

The motivation of the Seller is another huge factor in how quickly a business sells. A business owner that is ready to retire has made a plan. They understand that by the time they sell the business (8.2 months for argument's sake) and work in the business for another year, they are 20 months away from their daily appointment with the golf course and it cannot come soon enough!

This type of Seller will price the business right, put the work in to get through due diligence in a timely fashion and make the compromises and adjustments necessary to get the deal done. In contrast, with an unmotivated Seller who is just testing the market, there are just too many obstacles and the chances of getting to the end of the process are very low in the first place.

With that in mind, if a Buyer that makes an offer were to get to closing, here are roughly the timescales we normally see

1. Viewings and meeting Sellers - 1-2 months
2. Offers and negotiation to get to Heads of Terms (HOT) - 2 weeks
3. Due Diligence - 2 months (this varies greatly so just a ballpark average)
4. Contracts and eliminating contingencies, including funding - 2 months (this also varies greatly so just a ballpark average)

So if everything went according to plan and the sale was completed, the process on the above timescales would take 6 months. We have completed transactions that were 4 months from listing to closing day and the owner was on his sailboat full-time by month 6. It really does depend on a Buyer, Seller and the nature of the business.

There are many things that can slow the process down. Here are a few of the major ones we find:

- Seller not having financials ready or waiting on a year-end and then for the financials to be complete
- Buyers getting funding (contingent on the point above)
- Lease transfer and getting the landlord on board (generally requires paying landlord's solicitor fee, references and getting their approval)
- Getting franchisor approval (many will require a Buyer to go to training and be certified as well as pay a transfer fee)
- Slow legal council (this is a big issue that needs to be managed and can create weeks of delay towards the end of the process)

There is one final factor in both how long it takes to move through this process and increasing the chance of getting to the end of a successful close which is good process management. There are many moving parts, the parties have dozens of items they need to produce and do and there are many external people involved in the process which all need to be managed in a sort of concert.

The key to the optimisation of this process is a good M&A Advisor with experience in doing many transactions. At Transworld M&A we have well-honed systems that we can bring to bear, including virtual data rooms, due diligence tracking systems, document management, legal management systems, etc. Crucially, we have a keen ability to facilitate communication between all of the parties and keep everyone calm and on the same page.

Chapter 4 - Finding Business Sellers

Where and how do you find businesses for sale? This question understandably gets asked a lot and is fundamental to the process of buying a company. Buyer search can be one of the most time-consuming (and frustrating) aspects of the business buying process. We have had private equity companies tell us that they look at 100 companies for every one that they buy for example. The key is to focus, a good process, and persistence.

Transworld M&A are not Buyer side search agents so we do not get involved in doing specific searches for a Buyer beyond the listings we currently have which we are of course more than happy to discuss. There are specialist Buyer side search agents that focus on specific Seller search projects for Buyers and you can hire them for what is usually a monthly retainer and success fee.

If the Seller is not one of our listings, Transworld M&A get involved once a business Seller has been identified and qualified by the Buyer. We will be happy to reach out to the Seller and start the process of introductions and putting a potential offer together or join the process at any stage.

There are also business Buyer training programs that specifically teach business buying skills including how to source Seller prospects and create deal flow. In my opinion, the Business Buyers Club (BBC) in the

UK has an excellent program for new Buyers that covers this aspect in detail.

Therefore, we won't go into great detail on strategies around finding Sellers but for the completeness of this book, we have outlined some of the things to consider and some of the methods for finding Sellers below:

What Are You Looking for?

The idea of buying a small business can be exciting and daunting at the same time. While owning a business can be a lucrative investment and bring a sense of satisfaction and accomplishment, it is important to approach the process with caution and preparation.

Before you begin your search for a small business, it is important to determine what you are looking for. What are your goals for ownership? What do you hope to achieve through this investment? Do you want a business that provides a steady income, or are you looking for potential for growth and expansion? Understanding your goals will help you focus your search and make the right choice.

Once you have defined your goals, it is time to start researching the market. This will include finding businesses that align with your goals, researching the industry and market trends, and identifying any challenges and opportunities in the market. This information will help you make informed decisions and narrow down your choices to the best options.

We would suggest the following criteria as a starting point:

X-Factor Leadership/Sector Fit - Given the chapter on being the right Buyer, we would suggest it should be a business you are comfortable stepping into the role of X-Factor leader. This will in most cases mean a sector that you are familiar with and possibly have extensive experience. But the ability to take over a leadership should be paramount.

Geography - Is the business close enough to where you live given the amount of time you will need to spend on-site? It is generally very difficult to provide leadership without significant 'face time' with customers and staff.

Financials - Does the business look profitable? Is it growing? How much of the revenue is recurring/repeating? Are the financials up to date? Are there any anomalies on the balance sheet? Is the business capital intensive, do tangible assets need refreshing? How does seasonality affect things?...etc.

However, it is important to be comfortable at a high level with whatever business you are looking at. We do not suggest asking for significant additional financial information until after you get to meet the Seller. You may decide you don't like the vibe of the business, so more financial information is pointless anyway. Also, you may find more detailed information is not forthcoming and often meeting the owner is a much quicker way to get them to release key information.

Valuation - Is the business in the ballpark for what you think you can cash flow (see chapter on valuation). Can the business be grown to increase valuation?

Management Team - Is there a good team that can run the business day to day? Although we talk about stepping in for the X-Factor leader, few business Buyer actually want (or need) to be responsible for the day-to-day delivery, this is more about leadership so having a team in place that can keep things operating normally is usually key.

Motivated Seller - Is the Seller motivated? This is critical because if they are only half-hearted about selling the transaction is unlikely to complete as they will eject at the first difficult obstacle (see chapter 1 on why people sell).

Strong Key Value Drivers - See the chapter on Value Drivers.

Good Gut/Heart Feel - You as a Buyer have to like the business. There is something about having a strong feeling, a gut instinct, that is important. This is similar to when you know you have found the right house. If it doesn't feel right, it probably isn't. If it feels right, it could be a good candidate and this desire will carry you through the difficult periods.

Where Do You Find Business Sellers?

There are many places to find business Sellers. Below are a few of the more common examples:

Aggregator Websites - There are several websites where people list their business (i.e. businessforsale/Daltons/rightbiz/etc). People can list their business on these site although most often the listing is entered by business brokers. This can be a good way to find some types of businesses but there is a lot of competition, often the best business never make the websites and you need to work with the business brokers which can be challenging (more covered on this in a later chapter).

Physical Letters - This is one of the most effective methods, but it can be expensive. This method also requires a list of targets with up-to-date addresses.

LinkedIn - This can be very effective if you have narrowed down your target list. Sales Navigator (LinkedIn product) can help with this and LinkedIn has some great features to help with outreach. There are many good courses on the most effective use of LinkedIn.

Email - This can be effective, but people these days have so many emails coming in that often hiring a specialist email marketing company is the easiest way to use this medium. They will have the lists, understand how to avoid being spammed out and how to run a full-blown campaign.

Networking - This is one of the most effective ways to get leads if you are in networks with the type of targets you are looking for. Industry groups and trade associations are ideal. The key to this is to be very specific about what you are looking for (i.e. a CNC shop or electronics distributor) so people know who to recommend you to.

Business Brokers - Obviously business brokers see many businesses that are looking to sell and the larger ones have 100s of listings on their books. The challenge is that they also have 100s of Buyers every day enquiring about these businesses. If you can get friendly with a few brokers who understand what you are looking for, they can be very helpful.

Google - Google is very good for finding a list of specific businesses in a certain sector in many cases. Once these businesses are identified, a combination of the above methods can be used.

Buyer Search Agents - These are brokers who specialise in the Buyer search process. They can be very helpful as this is often a bulk numbers game which can be time-consuming. They generally charge a monthly retainer so it can get expensive.

Generally, many businesses will need to be approached and qualified so a good pipeline management system for 'deal flow' is essential. Again, it is not uncommon to speak with dozens of companies over many months before finding a good fit and then needing several of those to get one that makes sense and to get to the Head of Terms stage.

Chapter 5 - Connecting with
Business Sellers

Working with Transworld M&A

Transworld M&A will enter the process once you have identified and qualified a potential Seller. We will begin our process and help you with getting an introduction to the Seller, structuring the transaction, building trust with the Seller, getting through the Heads of Terms phase and then running the due diligence, funding and legal work streams for the several months afterwards. The objective is to significantly shorten the time this takes and increase the chances of it actually closing while making sure both sides are happy and trust each other, no small feat!

The First Meeting

Finding the right business to buy is very difficult and can be time-consuming as well as costly. Therefore, being prepared and getting the most out of a first meeting and maximising the chances of moving forward only makes sense. Like with all things in business, a little preparation and planning can go a long way.

The following section is meant to be quick and easy to read so has been organised in a series of points in a 'Do' and 'Dont' format. It is important to remember that this is a first date so all of the human aspects like first impressions, emotions, bias, etc. are more important than the technical detail. However, technical aspects can easily be misunderstood and misinterpreted at this stage, leading to negative emotions, so it is important to know how to handle them, which often largely involves acknowledgement but kicking potentially contentious points into a later stage.

The 'DO' List:

1. **Listen and deeply respect the person in front of you and their accomplishments** - Show Respect for their business and journey - Listen as long as they want to talk, for whatever they want to talk about. The longer they talk, the more they will trust you. The best way to get them talking is by asking them why they started the business and to share their journey. As a technical point, you will want to be very interested in why they want to sell and what their plans are afterwards.

2. **Share honestly and be yourself** - Business owners are savvy people almost by definition. They will appreciate someone who is genuine and spot anything fake or salesy and be put off in a heartbeat. Be Humble but equal - is a great expression that you also deserve respect but avoid stepping onto any kind of pedestal. Also, being positive is very important. Avoid talking about problems, biases, issues or too many weaknesses beyond a normal level of honesty. One can share honestly but be positive, even about lessons learned.

3. **Display business acquisition competence** - A Seller will probably have not sold a business and will be very nervous about it. If you give them the impression you have just shown up and don't really know what you are doing, it may compromise their willingness to move forward. Remember, there are many people that have gone through basic business buying training that have learned to talk the talk (although being a much more inferior Buyer to you in reality) that may be trying to speak with them. This doesn't mean you need to come

off as an expert, just that you have a plan, some basic understanding of the process (as in the previous section) and have made a business decision to do acquisitions. **A very easy shortcut is to say that *you realise you are not an expert but work closely with an M&A Advisor who will work with both of you to manage the process.***

4. **Understand the sharp edge of Legacy** - A Seller will say lots of things relating to getting the most money for the business as if that is all that matters. The reality is they are just going into a comfortable mode of selling a house or a car. However, when it comes to it, they are most deeply concerned about their legacy which is a combination of what happens to the people after the sale, the customers and the fact that this thing that they identify with is going to get bigger and better. Legacy matters to (almost) all of them. Therefore, it is important to give the impression that one of your overriding values is to honour their legacy and especially take care of their people who will be in an even better place potentially working with you. This may sound odd but most people selling feel there is more that could be done for their business and their people. When they meet a Buyer that gives them the impression can and will 'pick the ball up' they will be motivated to work hard on the relationship and transaction.

5. **Listen to their ideas about how the business could grow** - This follows on directly from the last point. They want their business to grow and be better, even if they don't own it because it is an extension of who they are. It is important to be excited about this and share your own ideas. The more you can get them into a mode of what post-sale will look like for the business, the more committed they will become to you. A very natural follow on is then to ask them what their plans are after the sale personally and become very interested in that. What

has now happened is that you are creating a joint future together.

6. **Appreciate their connection to their staff and customers -** They need to know their staff will be taken care of. These people have stood by them and they literally stand on their shoulders. Sometimes it is appreciation, sometimes it is guilt (as they have become wealthy and others have not) but generally discussing your excitement for having this kind of people on your team and what you can do for them will be viewed very positively. However, avoid being baited into any conversation about getting rid of anyone, this can often be a trap. You can just say... *it is not your policy to get rid of anyone, good people are hard to find, etc.*

7. **Be confident but vague about valuation -** Despite the above points, money does matter and they will want to know they are not wasting their time. If you waffle on this point they may think you are not serious. However, any attempt to discuss commercial terms in detail usually ends up acrimonious and is the number one reason for people falling out. Most Buyers and Sellers don't understand all the in/outs of deal structure, valuation, risk, etc and end up in a muddle focusing on the wrong points. Our advice is never to discuss commercial terms in specifics with a Buyer, let your M&A Advisor do that as they will have a process and can fulfil the role of an intermediary. However, what you can say is ....*that you understand that valuations are typically a function of EBITDA and a multiple and that you are fully committed to a transaction based on what is fair in both of these respects. However, both of these need help from specialists to work out exactly what they should be. Further, that you have an M&A Advisor and specialist M&A accountants that will help both parties work out what 'fair' looks like.*

8. **Be confident but vague on your financial resources** - They need to know you have the money (that you are not just a nice person but wasting their time). However, often Sellers don't understand the level to which we use debt to buy businesses and it can put them off early in the process. The best advice is to say that you have looked into this and have your own resources, can get a large credit line on your existing business and also have investors that have expressed interest and leave it at that. If they ask for more specifics, just say it will all depend on the opportunity and you would need to work with your advisors on a case-by-case basis.

9. **Address excess cash in the business head-on** - If they have cash in the business, they may be worried about that and it is very likely to come up. If they have a lot of excess cash (common) it could be more than the business is worth and handling this elegantly at this stage could put you in pole position. We realise there are some business Buyers who advocate for trying to manoeuvre around this topic and get excess cash as part of the sale. Our experience is that this is counterintuitive to Sellers (as they could just take a dividend) and engenders mistrust early. Again, our advice is not to go into detail but just to say something like: *we realise that your excess cash in the business is historical profit you have not taken out yet and belongs to you. We also know a business sale is a great time to extract that very tax efficiently. However, we would obviously want enough working capital (including cash) left in the business so it would continue to function after closing day. We have some very good advisors that can help us with this.*

10. **Key things you can try and gently understand but don't push unnaturally:**

    a. Why they are selling and their timetable as well as plans afterwards

b. The key people in the businesses who might carry on

c. Sales and profitability

d. Nature of their revenue/customers

e. Any gotchas

f. Debt and more detailed financial info if it is natural although this is often left for the advisors.

The 'DON'T' List:

1. **Get into any kind of detailed commercial discussion on price** - This is where people fall out. Leave this for your M&A advisor who is trained in how to delicately navigate this topic. Business sales are never a single price anyway, but a multi-faceted set of components.

2. **Get into detailed discussions about their staff and who would stay/go** - They may even ask you about this, but it can be a trap. Uneducated Sellers often have this fear that their company is going to be 'stripped' and it really makes them feel fearful and bad. They are trying to see if you are one of those people. Avoid this and emphasise the opposite if you can.

3. **Think of yourself as a 'Buyer' (with the implied rights, position and an unconscious Buyer pedestal)** - This is much more like a first date where you are exploring a deeper relationship so you do not want any air of superiority which could sour the relationship early on. Avoid the display of predatory thoughts or energy at all costs, they will pick up on this and no one wants to be 'prey'.

4. **Admit that you are financially challenged in any way** - Avoid showing weaknesses or talking too much about failures, this just plays on their mind later.

5. **Admit that you don't know what you are doing, are new to this, etc** - People are very nervous about selling their businesses and the last thing anyone wants to do is work with someone that doesn't really know what they are doing. The good thing is, most business owners don't know the detail about many aspects of their business (like doing accounts) but know how to manage the process and have employed the appropriate professionals to assist them. So assure them you do have a plan, resources, a strategy and the right people to get a fair deal for everyone (including their staff) done in a peaceful, timely manner. And of course, you have a qualified M&A Advisor who will make sure everything goes smoothly.

6. **Push or be rushed in any way** - Give them a feeling this will go at a natural pace that will be good for them and their business and do no harm. Remember, this is the biggest thing most people do next to getting married and having kids so there is a lot of fear and anxiety. The more you can calm and reassure them, the better it will go.

7. **Winging It by trying to do more of the process after the first meeting without help** - A good M&A advisor has training, processes, systems and extensive transaction experience. They navigate all the twists and turns of business sales on a daily basis and know where the land mines are. This is no different than any other profession where most people don't have extensive experience and end up learning by trial and error. This approach may be ok for some activities but in the M&A world mistakes can easily be made and tend to be significantly more costly than in most other areas of our lives.

Chapter 6 - Valuing the Business

Valuing a business is part of our everyday job as we obviously need to come up with a price to go to market and then set the business Sellers' expectations as far as what they are likely to achieve. When selling businesses, the basic premise is that the business is really only worth what someone is willing to pay for it of course.

There are other reasons for valuing a business like divorce, partner buyouts, debt financing, etc. but we will focus on what a business might sell for and how the deal might be structured as generally that is what most business owners are curious about.

Business valuation can be one of the most misunderstood areas of the process in our experience. Business owners tend to have all kinds of ideas about what their business is worth when in fact the simple premise for most (non-asset-based) business sales is that a Buyer is buying the future cash flow discounted by a % which takes into account risk, the time value on money and expected ROI.

Unlike accounting which is mostly mathematical and rules-based, business valuation tends to be 60% like accounting and 40% art or subjective. So there is an aspect that takes technical expertise to navigate and a significant portion which is opinion based.

Further, business sale transactions are not a single number, they are generally a collection of commercial terms from the closing payment, deferred payments, loan notes, excess cash, rolled equity, earn-outs, etc These all need to be factored in and applied against risk factors.

And then there are the banks. Most businesses are bought with some debt (like buy-to-let flats) so Buyers are relying on some lending. The banks will often only lend up to a certain point and actually not lend on transactions they feel have been overvalued.

Lastly and almost most importantly, the cash flow has to work. The debt paid back to the bank, any deferred payments to the Seller, additional costs post-sale like a new Managing Director or Finance Director, etc. all have to be manageable within the available cash flow. Otherwise, the transaction does not work with that particular Buyer despite all the philosophical arguments around valuation.

Many times business Sellers will mention that their accountant, financial adviser, Uber driver, brother-in-law, etc. said their business was worth X. Upon further investigation there was no method used for this option and in fact, none of these people is involved in daily working with buying and selling businesses in the real world. So the fact is there are methods and science that are helpful as at least as a foundation that gives us a starting point and a lens we can all work from.

An experienced business valuation/M&A professional can be very helpful to work through all the aspects of the valuation as well as work on the financial models (and negotiating) with Buyers and Sellers. But it is important to understand the fundamentals to participate effectively in the process and make sure they feel they are getting the right (a good) deal in their own mind.

Business Valuation Methods

There are basically three methods of valuation:

- Asset Method
- Income Method (Net Cash Flow)
- Market Method Using a Multiple

Asset Method - In general, small/medium businesses (under £50M) are valued on their ability to produce profit/cash flow and therefore we would use one of the 2 methods below and not this method.

The asset method is generally used where the assets are not generating a profit that is greater than their value. So for example, a machine shop is running break even or at a loss and it is sometimes better just to sell the machines and inventory rather than trying to sell the going concern with goodwill. Sometimes this can be morphed into selling a customer list or recurring contracts but inevitably we revert to one of the methods below as the value is determined by the profitability.

It is important to note that you choose only one method and do not add them together. So if you use the Market Method below you do not add the fixed assets on top of it. The reason is that the assets are needed to produce a profit. So, for example, you would buy a fish and chip shop for a certain ratio of the profit but you would expect the fish fryer, chairs, tables, refrigerators, etc that are used to run the shop to come with it and not suddenly be added as extras.

Income or Net Cash Flow (NCF) Method - This is probably the most accurate scientific way to value a business as you are taking the profit after tax cash and analysing that against a rate of return. This is very similar to how you would analyse a stock purchase on the public markets.

To calculate this, the first thing we have to determine is what the after-tax cash flow will be each year. Although business valuation is all about the cash flow to a Buyer in the future, normally we assume the business is going to run in a similar way as in the past. So we would generally take the last 3 years, maybe using some kind of weighting so that last year gets more emphasis than 3 years ago.

This cash flow would then be projected into the future and discounted back to a present value based on an expected rate of return call a 'discount rate'. Determining the discount rate is complicated and beyond the scope of this book but in general, for small/medium businesses, it ends up being mid-20s (i.e. 22% ish). This is generally the return an equity investor would expect on their investment or the cost of equity.

One way to visualise this is that it is similar to your home loan where the bank will give you £500K today for a cash flow of £2,000 per month for 30 years which is really £760K in total because of interest but the value today is £500K.

The good news for many people with glazed eyes at this point is that we don't tend to use this much in practice in the small/medium business arena as it is too difficult for all parties to get their heads around. But we like to explain it as it focuses the mind that the science part of the business valuation is a function of the business's ability to generate cash flow for a Buyer applied against an expected ROI/Risk factor.

Market Method Using a Multiple - The Market Method is the one that is generally used for profitable businesses when we work in the small/medium (under £50M) business arena. The basic premise is that we are comparing other, similar businesses that have sold based on some metric.

So a simple (but ludicrous just to make a point) one would be square footage. We could say that the last 10 fish and chips shops that were sold went for £500 per square foot of their shop. So if your shop is 300 square feet, we would say your shop would sell for £150K.

This is obviously much too crude so maybe we could next consider using revenue as the metric. The problem with revenue is that you can have one fish and chips shop on Oxford Street and one in the middle of nowhere, both doing £500K in revenue. Which one is the most valuable? Well, the one on Oxford Street is likely at a loss whereas the other one could be at a good profit due to drastically lower rents and staff costs so it would be more valuable as more after-tax cash would flow back into a Buyer's pocket. So revenue does not work that well in most cases.

We could use operating profit before tax as a metric. The problem is that different people put very different things through the company, many of which have nothing to do with the operations of the company. We notionally call these Ferraris and Hawaiian holidays as a tagline. Also, people do different things with salary and dividends as well as taxes so it is difficult to find commonality with just the Operating Profit figure on the annual report alone.

So the approach we take is to adjust this Operating Profit figure to calculate a number we call Normalised EBITDA (or NEBITDA). (EBITDA stands for earnings before Taxes, Interest, Depreciation and Amortisation).

The basic calculation is Normalised EBITDA * a Multiple.

What Is Normalised EBITDA (NEBITDA)

Normalised EBITDA is an attempt to ascertain what the profitability of the business will be for the Buyer post-sale before tax hence the term 'normalised'.

For the Normalised EBITDA calculation, we take the Operating Profit on the annual report and then 'add back' all the benefits that are going to the Seller. These can include the owner's salary (usually for 1 owner), director's pensions, director's cars and any other personal owner expenses. We also add back non-cash items like depreciation/amortisation and one-offs costs or loss of profit due to a fire or the company disposed of an asset. There also tend to be one-off adjustments for Covid impact and government grants related to the pandemic.

There are also often negative add-backs (or take-backs) that come into play. These occur generally to adjust the owner's salary for his replacement to a market wage as they may have been taking dividends instead of a salary. This also applies to other employees that have not taken a market wage or other staff that may be necessary for the business to continue (a CFO/finance function is common). Negative add-backs can also be generated from rent that is not at market rate and also capital equipment refresh costs that may be necessary in the future that have not been kept up to date in the last couple of years.

Further complicating the equation is what time period do we measure Normalised EBITDA for? The simple answer is that business valuation is based on the future cash flow so intrinsically we are trying to predict what future cash flow a Buyer will enjoy. However, historical financial performance is usually essential to determine what the future performance of the business will be.

What we generally <u>do not</u> do is just take the last 3 years and do an average. This would be saying that the performance 3 years ago was of equal value to determining performance as the previous year which for most SME businesses (especially those in growth) does not make sense.

With Covid, the results of many businesses in 2020/2021 have nothing to do with the future (some up/some down) so a view has to be taken. So there really is no correct answer for this that suits every situation and where the 'art' part of valuation comes in. The key is to keep the purpose of the exercise in mind which is to determine what the current run rate is.

Step 1 - Get the accountant's report for the last fiscal year - A good starting point is to look at the operating profit for the last fiscal year's accountant reports. This will have had adjustments done for accruals, work in progress, depreciation and other items that accountants tend to tidy up at the year-end.

Step 2 - Compile a list of add-backs for this fiscal year. These will include non-cash expenses like depreciation and amortization, bank interest on long-term loans, any costs that were non-operational to the business including the owners holidays/gym/car/house extension/family member on the payroll but not in business/etc, any costs that were one-off and will not recur like a fire or sometimes an experiment with a trade show and key employee. There are also negative add-backs (or take-backs) like normalisation of the owner's salary to a replacement cost and the same for anyone else in the business who is not being paid a market wage or is being paid through dividends (as they do not go through the P&L), normalisation of rent to a market rate, an estimate of capital refresh costs if the business has capital equipment.

Step 3 - Create a 'recast' by documenting all of these items on a spreadsheet with operating profit at the top and the list of add-backs/take-backs below. The sum of this is Normalised EBITDA for that fiscal period.

Step 2 - Get the previous 2-3 years' fiscal reports and repeat the process- This will start to give us an idea of growth and consistency.

Step 3 - Get the management accounts since the last fiscal year's accounts were prepared by the accountant. If this is more than 12 months, then we will want to 12 months since the last fiscal report taking us to the end of the most recent fiscal year + a separate report for the months since the fiscal year-end. We must keep in mind that these may or may not be accurate. There can be significant differences, especially for businesses like construction or that are inventory intensive and require stock/WIP adjustments at the year-end for example. So the idea is to get as much data as possible.

Step 4 - Repeat the recast process with the management accounts. - This may/may not be possible in a way that is accurate but the more data we have, the more patterns start to emerge and it allows us to take a view. Usually, the accountants will do a deeper dive in due diligence to come up with more accurate numbers which is why we tend to favour a Heads of Terms process that specifies formulas and not hard numbers recognising the calculation of Normalised EBITDA based on management accounts at early stages can be difficult.

We will now have a recast with the last 3 fiscal years filed accounts as well as current management accounts. There are many nuances and exceptions which we can help you with but this is the basic process. Once we have all of this data on a single spreadsheet, we can take a view and start to get an idea about what the profit streams of the business are.

What is a Multiple x

A multiple is then applied against Normalised EBITDA to come up with some idea of what to expect based on what others have sold for. But what multiple to use?

Many people throw out multiples as if they can be made up as some form of matter of opinion with no reference point. This is not true, we have many reference guides that do that analysis for us collating the data across 1000s of business sales so multiples are not just a finger in the air, there is <u>real data behind it.</u>

The next question is what drives these multiples. <u>The simple answer is RISK</u>.

A phenomenon of multiples is that as Normalised EBITDA rises, risk decreases and multiples tend to go up. Think of an aeroplane in turbulence. The larger the plane, the less it is affected. This is why a company with £300K Normalised EBITDA may have a 4x multiple and the exact same business with a £1.2M Normalised EBITDA might attract a 6x multiple. There is less risk of one or two things happening that derail Normalised EBITDA for the larger company so risk is lower.

I have done 100's of pricing exercises and found that in general:

- Businesses on the High Street with under £200K Normalised EBITDA sell for about a 1.5x - 2x multiple of Normalised EBITDA. (*Note: Often on the High Street we use a number called Sellers Discretionary Earnings (SDE) which is similar to the Normalised EBTIDA but we completely take out the owners salary and do not normalise an owner replacement with the idea the new owner will be taking the cash flow directly*).

- Most businesses under £1M Normalised EBITDA will attract a 3x or 4x multiple. Generally, if the business has recurring revenue and/or heavy equipment then this pushes the multiple up as risk is reduced.

- For a business that has Normalised EBITDA over £1M, the multiples tend to go up to 5x/6x.

- As EBITDA rises up to £2m/£3M/£4M, etc the multiple goes up again.

I have heard reports of brokers giving multiples far greater than these (sometimes triple!) but the data just doesn't back this up. Upon investigation, they are usually trying to persuade Sellers to pay a large upfront fee to sell their business and/or do not have the right education, experience and access to M&A data.

We always say that the multiple x is only the start of the conversation about valuation. The middle of the conversation is all the nuances for that particular business and the end of the conversation is whether the valuation created actually cash flows relative to the profit and debt ratios for a particular buyer.

A trained M&A Advisor would of course need to do a comprehensive review of each business as they are all different but hopefully, this gives you an idea. in the end, it is about whether a Buyer and Seller want to do business and are willing to go through the process of putting a deal together that works for both parties.

What About Working Capital and Debt?

Most businesses are sold on what the industry calls a 'debt free/cash free' basis. Ironically, this can be confusing as debts are left in the business to creditors and HMRC (VAT) and cash is left in the business in order for it to function so it is neither debt-free nor cash-free!

However, this is the industry terminology that is used and what it means is that there must be enough working capital in the business for it to continue operations at the normal level without the Buyer needing to add more. It also means that all the long-term debts (i.e. Covid Loans, long-term bank loans, etc as well as corporation tax) are part of the Seller's capital structure and need to be cleared on or before closing (or provision made to pay them as in the case corporation tax).

Clearing debt will obviously affect the cash that the Seller receives at closing as the debt will either be paid out of excess cash/working capital (see the chapter on working capital) or deducted from the closing payment.

However, these debts on the balance sheet do not affect the 'Enterprise Value' of the business. This is the ability of the business to generate profit, which is calculated by the various valuation methods. They are simply the way the Seller financed the business and will be cleared out of the Seller's funds (excess cash or their closing payment) at closing usually.

Normalised EBITDA Calculation Example

The following example is for a CNC machine shop in order to capture as many attributes as possible including capital equipment refresh:

CNC Machines LTD - Data Points

- Operating Profit last 12 months - £750K (for simplicity, we will assume this is known and just use this figure, typically this analysis is much more nuanced and we will look at the other periods).
- Owner takes £12K in salary and £80K in dividends. We have determined a reasonable market salary for his replacement is

£100K. The wife of the owner is also paid by the business but does not work in the business for £25K. The Owner also made a pension contribution of £40 during the year.
- Depreciation is £50K but the capital refresh expense (purchases going on the balance sheet to keep capital equipment productive) is £60K
- The owner has £60K of benefits including gym, a holiday and other non-operational expenses.
- The company did a trade show last year which was a disastrous one-off and will not be repeated for a cost of £10K
- The company had a legal dispute that has never happened before and is unlikely to happen again that cost £15K
- The Seller owns the property the business runs from through his pension and charges the company rent of £40K a year. However, if he sells the property he would like the new owner to pay £60K of rent per year.

Based on the above data, a recast would look like this:

- Operating Profit - £750K
- Add/Take Backs:
- Owner Salary - £12K
- Owner Pension Contribution - £40K
- Wife Salary - £25K
- Deprecation - £50K
- Other Owner Benefits - £60K
- Trade Show One Off - £10K
- Legal Dispute One Off - £15K
- Replacement Salary for Owner - (£100K)
- Capital Refresh - (£60K)
- Market Rent Normalisation - (£20K)

Normalised EBITDA using this period = £782K

As discussed earlier, this is just one data point and we would need to take a view on other periods. Also, when preparing a Head of Terms, it is often helpful to just include language like 'Normalised EBITDA to be agreed by both parties and then specify a multiple. This allows the accountants to have more data and more time to come to a conclusion during the due diligence process.

However, all parties will want some kind of estimate of what Enterprise Value will be so although the Heads of Terms may specify a formula, a working Normalised EBITDA number will generally be needed for conversation so an overall deal value can be estimated before the parties are willing to move forward. As always, there are many nuances to this and every transaction is different, but we will be happy to help work through this with you.

Key Factors That Affect Value

There are many factors that affect the value of a business. Some are subjective, some are objective. One of the most important things to understand is that the main mathematical premise is that a Buyer is purchasing future cash flow so the level of confidence they have in the business's ability to produce that future cash flow will determine the level of risk they associate with the business which will, in turn, affect the valuation equation and the multiple given is driven by risk.

A Buyer should also assess how easy it will be for them to take over the business, how well it fits into their portfolio, cultural fit, geography relative to where they live or the location of their other businesses as well as whether they like the business or not at a personal level.

Main Areas a Buyer Should Look at That May Affect Value:

Good Books and Records – Demonstrates the company is well run and they can rely on the financial data being disclosed.

Quality of Revenue – What are the chances the revenue (and margins) will continue as it has historically? This is why recurring revenue, long-term contracts, long-term customers, etc. will cause the multiple to go up.

Size of Normalised EBITDA – Mathematically valuation is often calculated as a multiple x Normalised EBITDA therefore the higher the Normalised EBITDA, the higher the valuation.

Key Man/Woman – The company needs to keep running and producing cash flow, people are most often key. If the owner leaves, does this create a risk for this cash flow? In an ideal situation, the owner will already have a management team and key people in place and a Buyer will assess there is little risk in a dip in operations.

Vendor Concentration and Dependency – If the company is heavily dependent on one or a few vendors this can be a red flag that increases risk. What happens if they decide to stop supplying? What about other contractual relationships that could suddenly disrupt business operations?

Documented Processes – Having documented processes versus a few people in the middle of everything to keep things going increases the confidence a Buyer has that the transition post-sale will be smooth. An operations manual that documents these processes is ideal. Also, most often Buyers know companies that are process based and well documented are easier to scale and grow.

The Above Aspects are Covered in More Detail Below:

Good Books and Records are Key to Selling a Business - During our training as business advisers and in all of our material we are told the three most important things to have ready when selling a business are:

- Good Books and Records

- Good Books and Records
- Good Books and Records

This is similar to the location, location, location mantra when selling real estate. Of course, it does not tell the whole story but the very experienced people who come up with this are just trying to make an important point that can not be overlooked in almost every circumstance.

One of the big reasons good books and records are so important is that businesses are generally valued based on their ability to generate cash flow for a Buyer in the future (see previous blogs for more details on this).

We have previously said that business sales are 60% heart and 40% head for a Buyer but the head stuff matters. This is similar to buying a house, you and your partner need to love the house but then the finances have to work, the kid's schools have to be close enough, work needs to be a decent travel distance, etc. You will never be able to buy the house if the payments are double your salary and the commute to work is 3 hours each way for example.

In a similar way, a Buyer needs to know that the cash flow produced by the business is going to be able to pay for any debt service, deferred payments to the Seller, enough for risk mitigation and still have enough left over for a Buyer to make a living if he needs to or enough of a return if he is an absentee Buyer.

I am always amazed at how some Sellers gloss over this point and think a Buyer will 'get' their business and think that the excuse of not being 'very into accounts' will somehow make poor or old books and records ok with a Buyer.

I can tell you from experience, it does not. If a Buyer does like the business and we proceed with due diligence, all that happens is that we get down towards the end and due diligence fails as a Buyer realises they cannot prove the cash flow...and we generally all conclude we have wasted several months and a Buyer should come back in 12 months while the Seller cleans up his books and records.

So what do we mean by good books and records? The following are the things we need for a good financial pack. They need to be accurate and up to date and provable in due diligence:

1. Filed accounts for the last 3 fiscal years (the un-abbreviated version of what is filed at Companies House) - this should be easy as the accountant produces these for every fiscal year end by law.
2. Management Accounts (Profit and Loss and Balance Sheet) through last month since the last year end (i.e. since the last filed accounts date) - These normally come out of the accounting system (i.e. Sage, Xero, QuickBooks). We do not expect the balance sheets to be accurate as the accountant will not have done any adjustments, but we can compensate for that when we do the recast for the financial pack.
3. Aged debtors and aged creditors (2 different reports) as of the last month - This comes out of the accounting system. Sometimes we need to wait for the bookkeeper to catch up with the last month end which is fine...we will wait.
4. Asset list over £5000 - This is a list of assets in the business with their market values (Seller estimate). This is not the book value with depreciation schedules, although these will be needed in DD. This is to ascertain the value of the assets in the business for valuation and for obtaining commercial lending.
5. Bank statements for the last 3 months - Self-explanatory and should just come right out of the online banking system.
6. VAT statements for the last 4 quarters - this will be available at the HMRC VAT portal.

There are a few notes to make on the above:

Businesses that have a lot of undeclared cash_- These will need special handling. We can help with that on a case-by-case basis. In general, the Seller needs to give a Buyer an idea of the cash they are taking and then he will need to prove this in due diligence, there are many methods for this.

Businesses that work on a % completion method (i.e. builders)_- These require the accountant to calculate the revenues, costs and WIP based on the progress of projects. Usually, they will do this twice a year so we may have to use previous financials and then look at cash flow, new contracts, etc. to ascertain the business is still performing at the same level. These businesses should have no problem producing the above reports but the profit (EBITDA) figures will need to be calculated by the accountant and we will come up with strategies during due diligence to work with this.

Businesses that take a lot of pre-payments spanning many months/years - Typically, we find the revenue and profit are recognised in a very conservative fashion to minimise tax. As with the above point, the accountant typically needs to come in and adjust the financials in order to reflect revenue and profits correctly. These are generally great businesses with recurring revenue, so worth the effort, but it is not as simple as producing an accounting system report.

Quality of Earnings - Valuation is mathematically based on Normalised EBITDA which in turn is driven by sales and gross profit. During the due diligence process, a Buyer will be determining what they think the ongoing EBITDA is going to be post-sale. This will drive the valuation, lending, cash flow, etc. Gaining confidence in this revenue stream is therefore critical.

A Buyer should assess the strength and predictability of the client base during due diligence. Generally, they will become uncomfortable if one customer has more than 15% of the revenue as this creates a big hole if this customer were to suddenly stop trading with the company, for example.

A Buyer should also be looking at debt collection. Customers that are not paying on time, especially over 90 days represent a risk that they may never pay at all or not pay the next invoices due to financial issues.

Long-term contracts are ideal but repeating customers who have been buying for a long time are also very good. Sometimes contracts create 'cliffs' where the customer will need to re-evaluate whereas a long-term repeat customer who is habituated to buying from the company could go on for years with no review...so it just depends.

The overall objective is to assess the likelihood that the sales volume will continue to drive the profit that the transaction is based on. Often if there is a concern about specific customers some of the valuations can be based on future collections as an earn-out and/or warranties can be introduced if customers were to disappear within an agreed time period.

Size of Normalised EBITDA - There is no getting away from the fact that Normalised EBITDA drives valuation in most transactions. It is important to remember that we are interested in future cash flow so at Buyer has to be confident that this will continue after they own the company post-sale.

The high the EBITDA, generally the lower the risk. The reason for this is similar to a plane in turbulence. A bigger plane is less buffeted by the winds than a smaller plane. Likewise, a company with a larger EBITDA or cash flows can withstand circumstances whereas a company with a smaller EBITDA may see its profit wiped out by a single event.

Therefore, not only is EBITDA critical in its own right for determining valuation but it is also linked to the actual multiple itself.

Key Man/Woman - Identifying who these people are is important. They should be operating as leaders and it should be evident that the Owner has backed away from the business as much as possible so they are no longer key to day-to-day functioning. We always say we like it when Sellers talk about how much golf they play or how many holidays they go on. This gives a Buyer confidence that the business can run without them.

The lack of a key person (s) once the owner leaves is one of the main reasons a financial Buyer (i.e. Private Equity) will reject a company for consideration. It is like having a plane with no pilot. It is generally very difficult to hire people from the outside into this position so this is generally not a viable short-term solution.

Documented Process - Many companies have few documented processes and rely heavily on a few individuals being involved to keep everything running. This is even more exacerbated when one of these individuals is the Seller. The problem with this is that if one of these people is removed for some reason, the business can suffer. This type of model is also not very scalable as it bottlenecks around these individuals. This creates risk (and hassle) for a Buyer post-sale which will often knock onto a business's valuation.

The solution to this is to move to a more process-oriented approach. One way to address this is to create an operations manual which documents all of the processes in the business. This exercise will force a re-evaluation and documentation of these processes often leading to natural efficiency improvements. The operations manual will also give a Buyer great comfort that the business can be understood and scaled beyond certain people. Also, in some cases, the operations manual can be used to 'franchise' the business to other locations.

This is a somewhat specialised area and we would normally suggest engaging a business consultant who can assist with this.

Vendor Concentration and Dependency - Some businesses are dependent on one or two vendors for the majority of what they make or sell. Should one of these relationships suddenly decide not to do business with them, it could have a detrimental impact on the company and cash flow. So a Buyer will want to assess this risk as well as the viability of replacement.

This can also arise in licensing situations like a franchise where the franchisor would cut off certain territories or products on short notice or even refuse to approve the sale full stop.

Risk can also arise where most of the revenue is from one or two suppliers who will continue to supply but there is a risk the product lines they supply will no longer be in demand in the future (i.e. fall out of fashion). In these cases, the ability and method to add new product lines must be assessed. Often this is a task done by the Seller historically so a Buyer needs to assess if they can learn the skills and build the contact networks necessary to keep a flow of new products being added.

Chapter 7 - Making Offers and Getting to Heads of Terms

At some point a Seller has been found and an initial contact made with a business that the Buyer is excited about. It is at this point we suggest that the Buyer contact us at Transworld M&A to assist with the rest of the process including structuring the actual deal and getting to Heads of Terms. It may have taken the Buyer months to get to this point and there are many ways that missteps could lead to a failure so getting the right help with save time, money and potential heartbreak.

Components of a Business Sale Transaction

Businesses are rarely sold for a single 'number' like a car or a house. It is a package of components that are unique to the business and the specific Buyer.

Generally, these include:

Closing payment - Cash paid by the Buyer to Seller at closing from their own funds or debt.

Deferred payments - This is a type of debt that is paid to the Seller over time, usually 2-4 years. The key point here is that it operates like debt and a Buyer has to pay it subject to warranties of course. These are a feature in the majority of business sales as they allow the business Seller to realise a higher value and also give a Buyer the comfort that the Seller is tied into the success of the business post-sale.

With deferred payments, a Buyer should expect the lawyer to add protections for the Seller who is now a creditor. Inherently the Buyer has a contract to pay the Seller so they have the normal rights of a contract. However, the lawyer may want to add other protections. These can include:

- Capital Controls which prevent any assets (including cash beyond what has been agreed) withdrawn from the business until the deferred amount is paid.
- A debenture over the business/fixed and floating charges (although if there is institutional debt, this is usually subordinated and not very valuable in practice)
- Share reversion where if payments are missed (i.e.maybe twice) shares start reverting back to the Seller (not desirable but just as a sort of penalty).

Occasionally there is a situation where the profitability of the business is volatile and the Buyer is concerned about the business down turning temporarily and there not being enough profit to pay the deferred. This can cause the Buyer to want to reduce the deferred to a safe level which is unacceptable to the Seller. A frequently used solution to this is to introduce the concept of 'Flexi Deferred' where if EBTIDA drops below the level the deal was constructed at, the deferred payment can be reduced for that period and pushed out into the future so it is not lost. This is what happens in practice anyway through negotiation, so it is sometimes better just to contractualise it at the legal stage. (Note: we normally recommend using a 'synthetic EBITDA' number that is derived as a historical percentage of gross profit. This prevents the Buyer from crushing actual EBITDA with admin expenses thereby reducing actual EBITDA.

Lastly, as deferred payments are effectively debt, the question of interest rates comes up. This is handled on a case by case basis and the most often outcome is that deferred does not carry an interest rate. Often instead, the inverse of Flexi Deferred is to pay out the deferred fast should EBITDA rise which is the most likely outcome. This is good for both parties.

Excess Cash - Surplus to operations Cash/Working Capital can often be added to the sale price and closing payment. This is basically profits the Seller has not extracted yet that are added to the sale value as a tax-saving mechanism. (see chapter on this subject)

Director Loan Write-Off - Often any director's loans on the balance sheet can be included in the business sale creating a Capital Gains Tax (generally 10% or 20%) effect instead of the Seller paying dividend tax which is normally declared to clear them at a year-end.

Earn Out - These are payments based on milestones. We usually use them for revenue/profit that is over and above what the Seller is paying for based on normal business operations and the calculations based on EBITDA that were used to derive the valuation.

Sellers Post Sale Salary- Generally the Seller stays in the business for a period of time and is paid a salary for doing so.

Shares in a Buyer's Business - Sometimes a Buyer includes shares in their larger entity as part of the compensation for the sale. This is most common where the Seller is going to stay in the business for several years after the sale so wants a piece of the action.

Retention of Shares in the Seller's Business - Occasionally the Seller will retain a small shareholding in their own business as a minority shareholder.

Retention of Business Units in the Seller's Business - Occasionally the Seller will keep certain business units and sell the other to a Buyer. Think of an alarm company that also does fire systems servicing. The Seller might sell the alarm contracts but keep fire servicing.

Sweet Equity to Key Employees - This is actual equity given to key employees from the Buyers shareholding. Generally, this is non-dividend bearing and means that the key employees that take the journey to the next exit (i.e. in 5 years) get a substantial payout. This is used extensively by Private Equity firms and we have seen 10%, 20% even 25% given. The key to this is 'leaver clauses' (as in leaving the business). These come into effect and the employee loses the shares in pretty much any situation where they have not worked through diligently without issue to the next exit. This is a very powerful motivator as the people feel like shareholders from day 1. Maybe more than a stock option plan or growth shares, which most people will put in the category of a lottery ticket.

Considerations When Constructing an Offer

Seller Orientation/Motivation - The first thing to consider when constructing an offer is how the Seller views the transaction. Are they very keen to sell (motivated Seller), do they have a timescale, do they need the money urgently or do they have plenty of money and plenty of time and just want a good Buyer for their business? This greatly affects how much the closing payment needs to be, how deferred will be paid, the appetite for risk, the plan for them existing the business, etc.

Valuation - What does the overall value of the business look like based on the valuation model (see previous chapter)?

Availability of Equity Funds - How much money do you as the Buyer have to put into the transaction? Keep in mind that you need to potentially budget at least £75K for costs such as due diligence review, funding, lawyer, etc.

Debt Required and Availability - Key questions are is this business fundable, how much debt is going to be needed, what type of debt is needed and how are the repayments structured? Also, at a personal level, are personal guarantees (PGs) needed and does the bank want some kind of 'hurt money' (Buyer introduced funds, typically 10%)? Details are covered in more detail in the section on debt.

Cash Flow Modelling - Doing a 3 year forward cash flow model including debt payments is critical. If it works (i.e. cash stays at comfortable levels every month in the future) we say the transaction 'cash flows'. If this is not the case, the transaction does not work and another deal structure needs to be found or the transaction abandoned.

Creating an Offer

The following are the steps for creating a commercial offer:

Step 1 - Determine the Normalised EBITDA of the business. This should be done over a time period that makes sense. In this step, you are trying to determine the run rate of the business currently so for some businesses this would be the last 6-12 months. For more long established businesses a longer time period may be appropriate but it is always about ascertaining the business's current ability to generate profit. Please see the chapter on valuation for a more detailed discussion on this.

Step 2 - Determine the multiple to be used. This was covered in a previous chapter but the rule of thumb is 3x -4x under £1M (mostly governed by the quality of earnings or recurring/repeat nature of the revenue stream), 4x to 5x to £1.5M and 5x to 6x up to £3M however this can vary significantly, especially as the normalised EBITDA rises and depending on the sector and risks in the business.

Step 3 - Determine the Enterprise Value (Headline Value) of the business. This can be as simple as multiplying the Normalised EBITDA * the multiple x.

Step 4 - Create a formula for any earn-outs. This is usually done when the Seller is insisting that the business will outperform the Normalised EBITDA in the first year. The basic concept is that if this happens, the Seller can participate in this excess as an earn-out which is contingent.

Step 5 - Note any long-term debt, director's loans and estimate what excess cash in the business might be (see chapter on working capital). An offer will simply state a formula but this will be used when explaining the offer.

Step 6 - Ascertain if the Sellers are going to leave any shares in the business. If so this becomes a partial buy out which has many implications including the need for a Shareholders Agreement (SHA) during the legal process but also how dividends will be calculated/distributed, any interest related to debt to by the business handled, the role of the minority shareholder on the board, etc.

Step 7 - Determine if the Seller is staying in the business and what their pay rate should be. This is normally a day/half rate for simplicity. A starting point is that any time spent by the Seller who is exiting for the first month is considered handover and not paid and any activities after one month are paid. This idea is it will be a mix of both and even out but this is a somewhat generic approach and every situation is different. Our experience is that exiting Sellers are cycled out of the business much quicker than expected during the planning phase.

Step 8 - Assess any special considerations that you would want documented at this stage. For example, will the owner's children agree to stay in the business? Is the offer contingent on certain events happening like a customer renewal or a certain profit level? etc.

Offer example:

Let's say Company A has the following data points:

1. 1. Normalised EBITDA for the last 12 months is £600K.
2. 2. The business is a maintenance business so highly recurring.
3. 3. The Buyer has £400K to invest in the transaction, £100K will need to be costs (funding, lawyer, etc)
4. 4. The Buyer is operating in a similar business and is local to the acquisition will become an additional business unit.
5. 5. We calculate there is £500K of excess cash in the business but £350K in long-term debt including accrued corporation tax meaning that £150K is net excess cash (Note: The actual figures will be determined at closing, this is just an estimate to give the Seller an idea of his cash flows).
6. 6. The director's loan account has a credit of £100K.
7. 7. The Seller feels the current run rate Normalised EBITDA is understated due to growth and will be £100K higher than the financials are showing in year 1.

An offer could look something like this:

Enterprise Value - £600K * 4x = £2.4M (4x as the revenue is highly recurring)

Purchase Price - £2.65M - Add: Excess cash of £150K and directors loan write-off £100K (both of these are added on top of the Enterprise Value and then paid/cancelled at closing which allows the Seller to only pay capital gain tax, they have no effect on the Buyer's purchase or on the Enterprise value..i.e. the Buyer is not actually paying for these).

Closing Payment - 70% of Enterprise Value = £1.68M + £150K excess cash + £100K directors loan write off = £1.93M

Deferred - 30% of Enterprise Value = £720K paid quarterly over 3 years so £240K per year.

Earn Out - 75% of amounts over £600K Normalised EBITDA in year 1, 50% year 2, 25% year 3. (Note: EBITDA will be constructed from a Gross Profit % to derive a 'synthetic EBITDA' post-sale for simplicity).

Excess Cash - The business will be sold on a debt free/cash free basis. Based on the balance sheet we have, this is estimated to mean £150K going back to the Seller at closing.

Director Loan Write-Off - Based on the balance sheet we have, there is a director loan of £100K. This will be effectively written off (there are some accounting choices here) at closing probably at 10% or 20% Capital Gains Tax (CGT) rates to be paid by the Seller rather than their normal highest tax rate (check with your tax advisor).

Does It Cash Flow?

Now we need to determine if the deal cash flows:

Step 1 - EBITDA is £600K - 25% tax of £150K = circa £450K of available cash.

Step 2 - Closing payment is £1.68M less equity investment of £300K = £1.38M cash flow lend over 6 years = circa £300K per year (this will vary depending on interest rates of course).

Step 3 - Deferred payment is £240K per year + £300K cash flow lend = £540K debt service.

In this case, the answer is NO...this offer does not cash flow. The £540K debt payments exceed the £450K which is available.

One way to make this work could be to:

1. Push the deferred payments out further if the Seller will allow it.

2. Negotiate a 'bullet' payment for half of the lend at the end of 5 years. This means half of the lend is interest only and is refinanced in 5 years' time.

With this in mind, the debt service could come down with deferred at £180K per year and bank debt service at £200K per year for a total of £380K. This is well below the £450K available so the deal now cash flows!

Just a quick caveat: this is a somewhat simplistic example for demonstration purposes. There can be many nuances such as the amount of money you need to take out of the business for your own expenses. But the idea is to provide some kind of framework for how this works. We would work with you in the detail on each individual situation as they are all unique with different risk profiles (i.e. with a very solid business with low risk you may be more comfortable with more debt, the opposite may be true with a higher risk business).

Presenting the Offer to the Seller

This is an important moment as if it is done correctly the Seller will be on board and the deal will proceed. Done incorrectly and the Seller may feel terrified, confused, insulted, angry or any combination and the deal will not proceed.

Our standard policy for presenting offers is as follows:

1. An offer is never sent in writing before the presentation. The Seller will never understand it unless they have M&A experience (just the terminology let alone all the mechanisms) and it will take longer to undo misinterpretations if we even get a chance.

2. We never let Buyers and Sellers talk about money. Transactions close because of trust and we have learned that conversations about money most often erode trust. We at Transworld M&A have a process, training and lots of experience presenting offers and dealing with objections so it is safer to let us do it.

3. We prepare a PowerPoint summary of the offer to talk through with them before leaving them with the hard copy. This allows us to talk through the main points in summary and then leave them with the detail. It is helpful to show them what their cash flows will be at closing with all the components as well as throughout the deferred period.

4. We allocate significant time to go through the offer and explain all aspects in detail, including how we got to the numbers. This allows the Seller to understand the mathematical nature of that and not revert into used car negotiation mode.

5. We invite them to comment when they are ready. This avoids putting people on the spot. However, we set the expectation that any counter-offers should have a mathematical basis and not just be some kind of negotiation tactic.

Getting to Heads of Terms

We use a standard Transworld M&A template for all of our transactions. This covers all the commercial points as well as non-disclosure, confidentiality and exclusivity. But makes the point the Heads of Terms is non-binding and does not have penalties on either party from leaving the transaction.

The reason for this is that if we have a good Seller prospect, it allows getting the Heads of Terms signed to be low risk for the Seller but gives you as a Buyer what you want which is exclusivity and a commitment level. If you start adding abortive costs, then the Sellers will take much longer, invite their lawyer in and want to have more discussion. All of this lowers the chances they will eventually agree to move to the next phase (negotiations can erode trust).

So a quick non-binding Heads of Terms is a very effective way of getting the Seller into the processes quickly and off the market. The Heads of Terms is generally just a DocuSign document for both parties. Once this is signed, the next phase begins, which is covered in the next chapter.

Just to acknowledge that there is another view that there is a significant amount of work that will go into due diligence and legals and if the Seller decides to stop the transaction just for their own reasons, they should reimburse the Buyer their costs. There is good merit in this approach in many cases and most private equity firms include abortive clauses with their Letter of Intent (LOI) which serves the same purpose as a Heads of Terms.

This approach makes a lot of sense in many situations, we have just found it can take longer and can lower the chance of getting a Buyer into the next phase as it forces detailed negotiation on price when data points have not been firmly established and trust has not yet been built through a process.

The Role of Transworld M&A in the Heads of Terms Phase - As we have mentioned, this is a companion book for our clients so it is assumed that Transworld M&A is managing all of the items in this chapter. The above is very much an overview and it would be almost impossible to put all the different nuances and variations that come up in constructing an offer and getting a transaction past the Heads of Terms phase.

Fortunately, we have the experience to manage this and can deal with (as well as have seen) most things that can come along. Also, at this stage, if we have done our job well, the Seller will start to see us as a trusted advisor/3rd party so we are able to have an independent dialogue with them to make sure they stay on track.

Chapter 8 - The Post Heads of Terms Process

The Heads of Terms (HOT) are now signed and both parties are ready to enter the next phase. This phase is the most complicated and lengthy and where the highest chance of failure is. Therefore, it is critical to follow a process and rely on your M&A Advisor to guide you through the process. Transworld M&A uses the Dynamic M&A Transaction Management Program (DTM) which has been developed over many years and 1000s of transactions. It has the purpose of getting transactions successfully to the closing table, as quickly as possible while building maximum trust between the parties.

What Happens The Day the Heads of Terms is Signed?

There are several things that happen to kick-start the process, the key is to create a quasi-formal container so that everyone knows what is expected and where the process is up to. Getting people to respond to requests and follow through is not a given (not even close in our experience!) so much of the process is designed to help with this.

There are three main benefits of working with us and letting us manage the transaction using our Dynamic M&A Transaction Management Program (DTM):

1. The chance the transaction closes will be greatly increased

2. The time it takes to close the transaction will be greatly reduced

3. The Buyer and Seller will be on a good footing for a good post-sale relationship

This system involves the following business/process streams which are managed separately:

1. **Due diligence** - Financial, payroll, IT, operational, legal, etc.

2. **Debt Funding** - All activities to secure any necessary debt for the purchase.

3. **Post-Sale Planning** - All activities and plans related to what happens from day 1 to 100 and thereafter.

4. **Legal** - The process of building up the document pack, working with the lawyers and all other legal issues.

Project Initiation

The following happens the day the Heads of Terms is signed:

1. **Welcome Email** - A welcome email is sent to both parties describing the process

2. **Virtual Data Room (VDR) set up** - Representatives (including accountants) from both parties are set up with Virtual Data Room (VDR) accounts although only the Seller will get access initially. (Note: A separate legal VDR will be set up for legal due diligence at a later stage).

3. **Virtual Due Diligence request list set up** - Buyer requests lists for the various due diligence types (i.e. financial, payroll, vat, IT, etc) are set up as spreadsheets with links so everyone has access and can see responses and progress.

4. **Weekly call set up** - 30 minute weekly team calls to track progress are set up at the same time slot on Zoom every week. These are one of the most helpful aspects of the process as it

gives people a chance to interact on a regular basis and solve any issue quickly.

5. **Lawyer introductions** - The bulk of the legal stream will generally start later but it usually helps to get the lawyer introduced and all the preliminary meetings and KYC out of the way so they are ready to go when the Buyers/Sellers are ready to move to this phase.

6. **Debt Funding introductions** - We will make introductions for the Buyer to funding specialists in our community for any needed lending.

7. **Due Diligence introductions** - We will make introductions for the Buyer to accountants that specialise in due diligence and business modelling in our community if needed.

8. **Seller Due Diligence Instruction Call** - We normally have a specific call to make sure the Seller knows how to use the Virtual Data Room and virtual request sheets and any other questions they may have.

9. **Buyer planning call** - We normally do a call to make sure the Buyer understands the process and ascertain what introduction would be helpful. We will also come up with a plan to get the most important information to progress any funding.

Due Diligence Stream

This is a very broad area and generally means the Buyer taking a look at the business from all angles and making sure they understand what they are buying. This generally breaks down as follows:

Financial Due Diligence (FDD) - This is what most people think of when the subject of due diligence is discussed. This activity means looking at all of the financial data of the company including historical financials, vat reports, payroll, leases, etc. More often than not, this is generally best done by an accountant that specialises in this. They will be able to tie everything together and know what they are looking for.

The data that is gathered in this stream will be used to validate the profitability of the company and allow us to calculate the Normalised EBITDA, Normalised Working Capital, excess cash, etc. which are the foundations for the transaction.

Tax Due Diligence - This is a specialised form of Financial Due Diligence (FDD) and will generally be done by the same professionals doing financial due diligence. We break it out here as it is critical that a Buyer understand the tax exposure from prior periods when buying a Limited Company so this aspect needs to be looked at by a specialist.

Legal Due Diligence - This aspect looks at all of the historical legal aspects of the limited company and any potential risks. Also, any new structures are evaluated in the same context. Similar to tax due diligence, this needs a specialist, as the impact is significant.

Operational Due Diligence - This is very specific to the company and also the Buyers requirements. This can be very broad but is basically the Buyer understanding how the business works and will work post sale and taking a view on it. This due diligence stream intersects with the Post Sale Planning stream and tends to be much more conversational and involves site visits, extended discussion and planning sessions.

Other Due Diligence Streams - Depending on the company, there may be other streams of work around the IT environment (which will check things like the software license situation), fixed asset (which will check things like viability/expected life), freehold due diligence (similar to when one buys a house), etc. The basic premise is that anything that needs to be checked that has an impact should be albeit in a way that balances cost effectiveness with risk.

Who Performs Due Diligence? - For the financial due diligence including tax and payroll, Transworld M&A will engage accounting specialists on their team to provide feedback, analysis and a report. For legal due diligence, this will be a member of the legal team. Operational due diligence is generally broad and has to do with the Buyer getting comfortable with the operations of the business in conjunction with post-sale planning.

Debt Funding Stream

Most businesses are bought we some debt. We always use the example of buy-to-let flats which most people understand. However, most business sales are not funded by high street banks but by specialist funders that operate more like investors than banks.

In fact, if you think about it, the business funders are really investors! They are putting money into the purchase of a business and getting an expected return rate via interest and a payment schedule that is made out of the profits of the business usually. The only difference with an equity investor is they do not have a payment schedule generally but have traded their investment for equity which will pay them dividends out of profit (rather than a set amount like a funder) and return funds to them upon some kind of exit.

But in the end, both are putting money in and expect it returned and a profit generated, it is just the method is slightly different. The reason for mentioning this is it sets the stage for working with these specialist funders and helps understand why they have the requirements that they will about how the transaction is structured and how the business will be run and by who.

Funding for a business purchase is obviously more complex than buying a property and generally requires a funding specialist that can manage the process. These specialists will know what funders are lending in what sectors as this can change like the wind. They will also know how to position your transaction in the most favourable way. They will also manage the relationship for the Buyer so they can stay focused on the details of the business sale.

Types of Debt Funding - There are several types of debt funding, we will cover a few of the more common types here:

Asset Funding - This is the most straightforward type of funding where the lender takes some of the assets of the business as a guarantee.

The most common assets that come to mind are heavy machinery, vehicles, excess stock or other hard items. However, if there is a default, liquidating these items is difficult and so the lender will generally only give a small % of the real value of these items as collateral, maybe 10-30% depending on the nature of the asset. Most businesses do not have these types of hard assets in any significant amount anyway so this type of lending is not that common in any significant amount relative to the size of a business purchase.

The biggest asset that is actually used as collateral for many businesses is the debtor book. The debtor book operates as almost cash as these outstanding balances will generally be paid in 30-60 days and turn into cash making this relatively low risk for the funder so the interest rates are lower and they are easier to get.

Typically a lender will lend between 50% - 85% of the debtor book balance depending on the perceived risk. For example, a company with debts to government entities that always pay their bills will be on the high end. A building contractor with a debtor book to mostly other building contractors will be on the lower end.

Debtor book financing generally does not involve the funder having any engagement with the customer or in fact, the customer knowing this type of funding has been implemented. This is important for most business Sellers as they will not want to upset their customer base.

One positive aspect of debtor book financing is that generally it operates like an overdraft and does not need regular repayment of capital. This is because each month the financing is renewed and basically pays off the previous month, so if sales are stable, only the interest is being paid.

The issue with this type of financing comes when sales are seasonal, cyclical or going down. What happens is that when the following month's debtor book is lower and is not as much as the previous month there is a shortfall. So the company has to find the cash difference elsewhere to continue operations if costs have stayed the same.

However, this type of funding tends to be the first port of call for Buyers as it is easy, less expensive and if discipline is applied, the balance can be slowly reduced over time. However, for the majority of transactions, this type of lending is not enough to make closing payments without significant Buyer capital being introduced to make up the difference. So this is often not a stand-alone solution for the closing payment so to speak but used in conjunction with other lending, most often cash flow lending.

Cash Flow/ Term Loans - These are loans based purely on the confidence the lender has that the business will be able to pay back the loan out of profits. The rule of thumb is that a lender will lend up to 2.5x normalised EBTIDA generally over 5-6 year period with capital and interest being paid back as part of the payment plan.

The interest rates tend to be quite high, but when taken in the context of the very high returns of owning a business, many Buyers will conclude it to be a worthwhile mechanism for getting a business they want to acquire over the line. Many lenders will offer a 'bullet' payment on a large portion of the capital portion of the loan (i.e. 30%-50%) payable at the end with only interest due during the term on that portion. This can be exceptionally helpful for cash flow and the bullet is generally simply refinanced at the end of the loan term.

As the lenders are lending on 'cash flow', you can imagine they are very interested in how the business is going to operate as demonstrated by a good business plan. These business plans must generally be constructed by a specialist but are good to have for running the business anyway, so tend to be a good investment. Transworld M&A will assign one of our business modelling specialists to build the model in conjunction with doing financial due diligence.

These lenders will generally also want to know that whoever is buying the business has the experience to run the business successfully. They are also familiar with the X-Factor leadership void that can be created when an owner leaves and want to make sure that is addressed and the business will continue to be profitable so payments can be made.

The lender will also generally want the Buyer to have skin in the game and ask for a certain % of the initial capitalization of the transaction (i.e. closing payment to the Seller or investment in the business) to be paid out of the Buyer's equity funds. This tends to be 10-15% of the funds lent for example. They will often also want Personal Guarantees (PGs) from Buyers although these may not be for 100% of the loan and can be temporary. A lending consultant can help with all of this.

These types of loans can make or break deals due to the amount they are willing to lend but of course, the capital + interest due can be a huge strain on cash flow so understanding whether this is viable is critical (this is covered in the chapter of deal structure).

Government Backed Loans - There have been several government backed loan schemes, especially during Covid, that were very helpful in acquiring businesses as they reduced the risks for the banks so made them easier to get. These loans generally worked like term loans above with capital and interest paid over a period of time but did not require PGs below £250K for example.

This type of loan still exists but with many constraints, so few people use them at the time of this writing. If you work with a lending consultant, they will be able to advise what is on offer in the market at the current time.

Others - There are other ways to get debt including a wide variety of structures that can be used with private individuals. We have also seen some Buyers work with HMRC to delay tax payments with Time To Pay (TTP), work with the Seller to use their excess cash and basically turn them into a bank (most Sellers are not willing to do this as the risk profile greatly increases at a time they are looking to move on from the business), make deals with specific suppliers in trade for equity, etc. So, like everything else in the M&A, there is a normal framework and then many exceptions limited only by the creativity of the team involved in the transaction.

Post-Sale Planning Stream (The Fun Part)

Much of the business sale process is technical, stressful, and necessary, but boring and downright tedious. However, the exception is often where both parties get to build a new future for the company and themselves.

During this phase, the Buyer will start working out what everything is going to look like starting on day 1. Often they notionally talk about the first 100s days just to make the exercise look manageable but in reality, this is the foundation for the future of the company.

For the Seller (and any staff involved) this can be a very enjoyable process as they have new ideas and new energy and may be doing the things they wanted to do but didn't have time or energy. We have seen situations where Sellers fall back in love with their business during the process and pull out of the business sale as they want to do it themselves!

We suggest that the majority of the post Heads of Terms efforts by the Buyers and Sellers are spent on this activity while the advisors focus their time on the other streams. This really allows the Buyers and Sellers to get to know each other and get comfortable with the business and the future together. If this doesn't go well, of course, it generally means the deal should not proceed as this is not a good 'cultural fit' which is the number one reason that deals don't close or fail to deliver if they do.

We don't have any guidelines for this process as we have found the Buyer and Seller generally make their own plan quite successfully in each situation. The only suggestion we have is that specific activities and conversations are designated for 'post-sale planning' and that other aspects of the due diligence process are not covered, especially anything around commercial terms or legal aspects. The reason is that these can tend to be quite stressful and without advisor help, conversations can easily go in the wrong direction and spoil what was otherwise a very productive, inspiring meeting.

Legal/Contracts Stream

Managing the legal process can be one of the most stressful parts of the business sale process. This is the part where everything that has been agreed has to be put into a contractual framework. This generally comprises about 15 documents, the main one being the Share Purchase Agreement (SPA) (Asset Purchase Agreement if this is a purely asset sale which is not common). If the Seller is leaving shares in the business or if there are multiple shareholders then the Shareholder Agreement (SHA) also becomes a point of major focus.

In addition to putting the transaction parameters into legal documents, during the legal process, the Seller will also be asked to give warranties and indemnities. These allow the Buyer recourse if certain things are not disclosed and cause a problem or certain things happen where the genesis was when the Seller owned the company. An example would be a tax warranty where the tax man found an error in a previous year and levied a fine for that prior year after the business sale.

Part of the disclosure will also be a Disclosure Letter where the Seller is guaranteeing everything that has been disclosed which is accompanied by a Disclosure Bundle which is all the items/documents that have been disclosed. This Disclosure Bundle is produced out of the Virtual Data Room (VDR) which will explain why we are so insistent during the process that all disclosure go to the VDR and the virtual request sheets and not through email or some other means as it creates a nightmare at the end for the lawyers to chase down all the disclosure.

We must also remember that each lawyer works for their clients best interest. We normally work with lawyers in our community that understand that a business sale transaction is more like a wedding and not a divorce (most don't understand this as much of law is inherently confrontational). However, as with any marriage, both parties have their points of view that must be reconciled. When you factor in warranties, commercial terms, post-sale terms, loans, risk, etc....it can get very multi-dimensionally complicated, tense and tempers can fray. It is often helpful to remember that this is normal and the advisors are here to help you get through the process, as others have done before.

At this point, it is worth repeating that time matters! We have now decided to do the deal so every day of delay costs the Buyer money in lost profits. How much? Well if after tax profits are £520K a year, for example, it is £10K a week! So good project management is key and minimising 'drift' is very important. You might expect as we are explaining this, we are hyper-focused on minimising drift and getting to the closing table as quickly as possible.

We find the key to project managing the legal process is to focus on the fact that it is really about building up a set of documents that both parties can sign. the way to project manage this is to understand what the state of these documents are, who has them, what next, what are the outstanding issues, etc.

We have created a Legal Management Dashboard that just does that. Once the legal process starts, we will generally invite the lawyers onto our weekly calls and review this dashboard so everyone knows where the project stands.

This is not an exhaustive list but covers most of what is needed:

Acquisition Documentation

- Share Purchase Agreement - Main purchase document
- Shareholder Agreement - All encompassing agreement for post-sale relationship if multiple shareholders
- Disclosure Letter - Disclosures by the Seller including Disclosure Bundle
- Seller Consultancy Agreement
- Board minutes of Target - approving the share transfers, PSC changes; appointment of director
- Board Minute of Buyer - authorising the acquisition and entry into the SPA
- Resolution of Buyer to amend articles for sole director provision
- Stock Transfer Form - For Companies House filing

Companies House Filings

- AP01 - To appoint an individual as a company director
- PSC07 - To notify Companies House that a person or entity is no longer a Person of Significant Control (PSC), Relevant Legal Entity (RLE) or Other Registrable Person (ORP)
- PSC02 - To give notice of a relevant legal entity (RLE) with significant control

Completion Deliverables

- Statutory Registers and Minute Books of – Common seal, minute book, certificate of incorporation and change of name, etc.

- Login details - In the agreed form relating to each of the Seller's social media accounts (if any), website, and other marketing sources or portals

- Employee Details - In the agreed form in respect of each of the Employees

- Insurance Evidence - Evidence in a form satisfactory to the Buyer that appropriate insurances have to be obtained (and paid for) in respect of the Seller's employers liability insurance, directors' and officers'

- Release Evidence - Evidence in a form satisfactory to the Buyer that all guarantees, bonds and indemnities, securities or Encumbrances given by the Sellers relating to the indebtedness, liabilities or obligations of the Seller or any person connected with the Seller have been released.

- Sellers Bank Account - A statement for that account as at the close of business on the Business Day immediately before Completion; a copy of the mandate for that account; and all chequebooks in respect of that account;

- Balance Sheet - A balance sheet in respect of the Target as at close of business on the Business Day prior to the Completion Date

- Bank Cards - All credit, debit or other cards in the name of or for the account of the Sellers in the possession of any person resigning from an office or employment on Completion

- Companies House Details - All Companies House web filing service details for the Company, including the relevant sign-in e-mail address, security code and company authentication code

Post Completion

- Stamp Duty payment to HMRC

Getting to the End

Generally all of these streams of activity run in parallel. The only exception is that we tend to bring in the legal team about halfway through when it feels like the deal is on solid foundations.

The key is to work through the process, be patient and keep communicating. Certain periods can be very stressful and there will be many problems to be solved. Most issues can be resolved on the weekly calls. More serious issues can be taken offline and we will work as an intermediary with the relevant parties to work through any issues in a cooperative, creative fashion.

Deal Fatigue - This is a very real phenomenon in which almost no Buyer or Seller escapes. The final stages of a deal can be very tedious and stressful as there is so much at stake. There can often be delays caused by minor issues or occasionally major issues coming up right at the end. Regardless, it is important to understand that deal fatigue will happen at some point and not to panic or make any rash decisions. Our advice is to acknowledge it and keep in mind that the deal will eventually close and these particular issues will disappear and just keep going as the end is right around the corner!

Chapter 9 -

Determining Working Capital

and Excess Cash

Determining the right level of working capital and excess cash distributions to the Seller is a critical step in the business sale process. This discussion can often be robust, as it has a direct ££ impact on both parties at closing. The Buyer wants to make sure the risk of running out of money is low, the Seller wants as much as possible as what they will often view as their money!

The challenge is that the calculations are often highly technical on one hand and driven by the accountants. On the other hand, the final formula is a matter of judgment on which the Buyer and Seller must come to an agreement. Our advice is just to realize this is a challenging discussion, work through it methodically with the right advice and professionals and realize there will be some give and take that does not really include anyone winning or losing but just different lenses.

Terminology

Cash Free/Debt Free

Most businesses are sold on a debt-free/cash-free basis. What this means in practice is that the long-term debts, including accrued taxation, are covered by the Seller either out of their existing cash or closing payment. This also means that any excess cash is returned to the Seller as this usually represents profit that has not been extracted yet. However, usually, there is the expectation that a reasonable or minimal amount of working capital (and cash) is left in the business so it can operate under normal conditions.

Excess Cash

Excess working capital generally manifests as excess cash in the business, so this is what most people relate to as it seems intuitive to watch a bank balance grow to more than is required for the business to operate. However, it is necessary to factor in all the requirements for cash in a business, especially outstanding and/or upcoming debts like bank loans and taxes in order to get an accurate picture. For this reason, a proper analysis of 'working capital' is necessary. This also needs to take into account seasonality and other time-related aspects of the business cycle.

Excess Working Capital

Generally, excess working capital exists in a business as profits have been accumulated that have not been reinvested, paid off debt, or taken out as a dividend. These accumulated profits are considered excess to operations (not needed for the business to produce the cash flow) and could be removed via dividend prior to a sale without impacting the viability of the business (although this may not be the best method from a tax perspective as below).

This means the fixed and net current assets (i.e. debtors, stock, creditors, etc. and a minimum amount of cash) on the balance sheet are what is transferred. Just specifying 'cash free/debt free' is generally too simplistic as it does not take into account things like debtors/stock turns and when creditors are due that could require cash in the bank.

For example, what would happen if the Seller got all the customers to pay early so that on closing day there were no debtors and just cash in the bank which the Seller would sweep out? The Buyer would be left with creditors but no customer receipts to cover them. Hence the analysis of working capital compressively is more reflective of the nuances of cash flow. This is covered in more detail below.

Tax Considerations

Once an estimate of the Excess Working Capital is calculated, it is technically possible for the Seller to extract this from the business prior to the sale as a dividend without harming the operations of the business. However, this will generally cause a tax event for the Seller with many paying 40%+ in tax on this extraction.

Often a more tax-efficient method is to add the excess working capital to the business sale value. This means the Seller is then only taxed at Capital Gains tax rates (usually 10% under £1M and 20% over £1m per person currently in the UK). The effect is that of the Buyer 'buying the excess cash from the Seller'. (Note: This is just meant to be for discussion, each Buyer/Seller should check their individual situation with their tax advisor).

Long-Term Debts

Generally, long-term debts need to be paid off prior to closing as they were part of the means the Seller used to finance the business. These include things like Bounce Back loans, Funding Circle, bank loans, etc. Often what looks like excess working capital is simply these loans that are still in the bank account so to speak and need to be paid back. If there is not sufficient cash in the business to satisfy these loans, usually the Seller's closing payment is reduced and the Buyer takes on or pays these loans with those funds.

Director's Loan Accounts (DLA)

A business sale can often be an opportunity to have DLAs cleared and only incur capital gains tax (CGT on business sales is 10% or 20% at the time of this writing). DLAs are money disbursed or payments made to the directors that are not payroll and are not operational to the business (i.e. such as business expense reimbursement).

Typically, the DLA account is used as a sort of placeholder for shareholder disbursements and is turned into dividends by the accountant when the year-end accounts are done. DLA's must be paid back within 9 months of the fiscal year-end or a tax must be paid by the company (32.5% at the time of this writing). When a business sale transaction happens, the Seller can declare a dividend prior to the business sale to clear the DLA but this can often attract 40%+ tax depending on the amount.

Alternatively, the DLA can be paid back on the day of sale from the proceeds of the closing payment. This, in turn, becomes excess cash which is returned to the Seller on closing day and in effect increases the sale value hence attracting only the capital gains tax amount. As always, advice should be taken from an appropriate tax advisor as there are nuances.

Calculating Working Capital (Net Current Assets)

Working capital is the current assets and liabilities of a business that continuity goes up and down as the business continues to operate. The elements of working capital are like a piston that goes round and round with one side high and another lower only to switch back but always maintaining a balance and momentum.

The common elements of working capital on the balance sheet are below:

Current Assets

- Cash

- Debtors - customers who owe the business

- Stock

- Work in Progress

- Pre-Payments – Money the business has paid in advance

Current Liabilities

- Creditors – suppliers to who the business owes

- Payroll taxes owed as of now

- VAT owed as of now

- Accruals – Money the business owes but creditors have not invoiced

- Corporation tax owed as of now

- Customer deposits

- Other cash and short-term debt items

Note: We normally exclude the Director's Loans and Inter Company Loan accounts for the working capital calculation as the assumption is Director's Loans will just be turned into a dividend or written off at closing and Interco Loans are written off so have no impact on cash flow.

An example of a working capital calculation for Best Body Whole Foods would be:

- Cash - £350K

- Stock - £150K

- Debtors - £400K

- Trade Creditors - (£350K)

- VAT (£150K)

- Payroll Taxes (£10K)

- Corp Tax Accrual (£90K)

Net Working Capital = £300K

Calculating - Normalised Working Capital/Target Working Capital/Working Capital PEG

These terms are generally used to mean the same thing. When all the working capital elements above are aggregated (added up), this number is what we call net working capital. If the net working capital becomes too low, the business feels like it is under pressure normally manifested as not having enough money to pay creditors or payroll when they are due. At some point, this will need to be rectified by injecting more cash (working capital) into the business via a loan or capital from the shareholders.

A business Buyer expects to purchase a working business that will not need more cash injected later so it is important to determine a minimum working capital to avoid this. One of these three terms is generally used to denote what this number is.

There are several methods for determining what a minimum working capital figure should be although there can be many nuances depending on the business:

Average Working Capital Over a Twelve-Month Period - In this method, the average working capital over a 12-month (or agreed) period is examined and the average is set as the minimum working capital figure. The challenge in this method is to determine how much was excess during the 12-month period. Often cash is excluded or minimised for this calculation for that reason.

One caveat is that if the business is in growth, it will require more working capital so the prior year will not be indicative of the current run rate and/or need to be adjusted. Also, seasonality will need to be taken into account so the business does not run low on working capital during quiet months.

Low Water Mark Working Capital Over a Twelve-Month Period

This is similar to the above method except the lowest figure is taken representing the lowest that the business is likely to go. Again, the challenge is to determine what a reasonable cash balance would be as more than likely excess cash existed in the business at that point.

Net Current Assets at Zero - In this method, it is assumed that the business is cash generative so having current assets and liabilities balanced to zero will result in a situation where the business will not run out of cash. This often works well as the current assets in the form of debtors are often collected faster than many of the current liabilities need to be paid, especially items like corporation tax so the business is always ahead so to speak.

This can work well for some businesses but fall over for others that have very slow payment terms from customers or long lead times from stock purchase to a stock sale. This also can become unworkable if growth is steep, which requires more working capital to keep up.

Cash Flow Modelling - In this method, a cash flow projection is constructed over at least the next 12 months but generally longer. This will allow a clear view of what excess working capital manifesting in cash is over a longer period and allow a clear view of what cash could be taken out at closing without causing the cash balance to go dangerously low in the future.

This is often the method easiest for both Buyer and Seller to understand but requires a focused project working with both sets of accountants. One caveat of this method is that the Seller is selling the business as it is running today. If the Buyer wants to grow it this is great, but it is not up to the Seller to provide working capital for them to do so.

Others - The objective of determining a minimum working capital level is that the business does not run out of money at some point in the future based on the current operating level. Often there are many technical nuances that require the Buyer and Seller's accountants to come to a joint conclusion using a hybrid of these methods.

Methods for Managing Working Capital During a Business Sale Process

Closing Accounts Method - With this method, a target working capital figure is specified either at the Heads of Terms/LOI stage or at some stage during the Due Diligence phase. Again, getting the parties to agree on this can be contentious so the assistance of a qualified M&A Advisor can be helpful in managing the discussion. It is unlikely that both sides' accountants will agree on this figure and there are likely to be philosophical differences on what constitutes working capital. However, at some point, a figure that the Seller is committing to the Buyer will be on the balance sheet on closing day and must be agreed upon.

Once this figure is agreed upon and the business sale closes on a particular day (month ends are easiest), the accountants will need a period of time (i.e. a month or two) to determine exactly what the balance sheet was on closing day which we call preparing closing accounts. The working capital figure on this balance sheet is compared to the target working capital figure and any overages are paid back to the Seller and any underages are generally deducted either from any closing payment retention or the Seller's next deferred payment.

Typically on closing day, the amount of excess cash will be estimated and a 'retention' (i.e. 10%) will be held back and the balance paid to the Seller with the closing payment.

This method is often used when the transaction is simple and the professional accountant's and advisor's time on a transaction is minimal. This is because there are just two points where analysis needs to happen around the working capital figure and then the preparation of the closing accounts. These can easily be done by the incumbent accountant as discrete projects.

Lock Box Method - With this method, an offer on the business is made based on a specific balance sheet, usually the last year-end filed accounts. This then becomes the 'effective date' with the purchaser taking on the risk of the business's performance from that date.

The Seller is then contractually obligated not to take resources out of the business (i.e. cash, dividends, equipment) beyond the 'leakage' that has been agreed with the Buyer. They are also under constraints to run the businesses normally on a day-to-day basis and not make any major capital expenditures, commitments for staff, inventory changes, etc. without the consent of the Buyer.

If the period between agreeing on the offer and closing is lengthy, the Seller will want the benefit of the profit generated during that period and can agree to adjustments at closing often called 'stub' payments.

The advantage is that it eliminates the uncertainty and post-sale efforts involved in producing closing accounts. The disadvantage is that the Seller is constrained in running their business and if the transaction does not close they could lose momentum during that period when they may have made other investment decisions, etc. It can also become very complex to manage over the due diligence period to ensure there are no anomalies so generally this requires more advisor time and focus.

Chapter 10 - What About Commercial Property?

Many businesses have commercial property (s) that is owned by the business. This can be the office the business is run from, a factory or warehouse used by the business or even an investment property not related to business operations.

One way commercial property can be looked at is profit that the Seller did not take out as dividends but invested in commercial property inside the business. This would not be that different than if they had invested in stocks/bonds on the balance sheet instead of taking dividends. An argument can then be made that this 'frozen' profit should therefore be returned to the owner at closing in a similar way to excess cash.

Alternatively, if the property is appropriate and functional for the business, it can be viewed as any other cash producing asset such as a machine which drives EBITDA and is, therefore, part of the balance sheet delivered to the Buyer at closing.

There are generally two ways of dealing with this commercial property:

1 - The Property is Removed (de-merged) from the Company Prior to Sale and Rent is Added

This is the most common scenario as most business Buyers do not want to buy real estate. An exception can arise if the property is a small office of not much value for example. (The reason is that buying a property takes cash for the deposit (i.e. 25%) and the returns are far less than buying businesses). The Buyer would often prefer that the property is removed from the business prior to the sale.

The issue arises that removing the business generally creates a Stamp Duty charge as the property would conventionally be 'sold' to the Seller personally or another Seller company. This tax can be significant so the Seller will want to avoid it. The solution is a 'de-merger' where the property is moved into another company in the group which is then moved or de-merged out of the group. This requires a specialist lawyer and HMRC approval and a certain lead time but is a very common approach.

When the property is taken out of the company generally this will create a rent requirement that the company must now pay to the new owner (the Seller personally or his new limited property company). This was a cost that was not on the P&L previously and therefore reduces EBITDA which will likely have an impact on valuation and also on the available cash flow post-sale. So an evaluation must be done about whether the reduction in valuation is offset by the value of the property being taken out to make it worth it so to speak.

2 - The Property is Left In the Business

If the property is left in the business it would seem at first glance that there is nothing to do as it becomes part of the asset base that generates cash flow and the value is reflected in EBITDA and the valuation. However, this is not necessarily the case as often the property value (bought with the owner's profit) far exceeds the value of the cash flow being created.

In this case, a common approach is to determine the market rent value and also the market value of the property generally through a survey (often 2 or 3). The rent would then be subtracted from EBITDA rolling through to a lower valuation but then the property value would be added back into the valuation.

Another way to visualise this is if the property was not part of operations at all but a pure investment and was staying in the business it would clearly be the owner's profit that would be in addition to any goodwill value.

Part of the contract package at closing would include a long-term lease on the property to the Seller's company.

Additional Considerations

Property often has a mortgage attached to it. So it is important that these calculations are done net of the mortgage of course as this is the actual Seller equity in the property.

Often the mortgage can be used as part of the debt financing package for the business. If there is no mortgage, generally the Buyer can get quite a large loan against the property (i.e. 75%) if it is staying in the business and this becomes part of the funding package.

There can be other issues with a property that need to be considered like any liens that might exist, government mandates that might be due/coming in the future, changes in the tax regime and/or zoning, etc.

Chapter 11 - Confidentiality

Matters

When a Seller agrees to engage a Buyer there is a huge leap of trust that is taken as they will be disclosing not only the fact they are for sale but details about the business that could be used by a competitor or just inadvertently shared with the community which would impact their relationship with customer, employees and supplies. It is therefore critical for a Buyer to honour this trust and the Non-Disclosure terms that were signed before engaging with a Seller.

When most people decide to sell a major asset like a house or a car there is generally an advertising process to make as many people aware the item is for sale as possible. This can even include putting a for sale sign in front of the house or a notice inside the car windshield for example.

In the case of selling a business, this community advertising approach would have many negative consequences. Because of this, the normal advice is to tell as few people as possible the business is for sale and only reach out anonymously. The following are some of the groups and reasons for this anonymity:

Customers - If customers know a business is being sold, they might make many negative assumptions like there is a problem with the business and better to find another supplier as quality might go down, etc. They could lose money if you suddenly go out of business and they have outstanding orders, deposits or you are about to become unreliable, etc.

Suppliers - Similarly, some suppliers are strategic and may look for other outlets in the Sellers area. Also, they could try and poach staff or modify payment terms if they think there is a financial risk.

Employees - This is generally the last group a Seller wants to know your business is for sale. In fact, we recommend not telling the employees until after the sale is made. The reason is that many business sales fall through and this can create all kinds of problems with staff morale.

Just knowing a business is for sale can make people insecure and they will start looking for other jobs. After the sale is complete, this is a different story as we can generally position the Buyer as an investor and tell the story about how everything is now going to be bigger and better, etc.

Competitors - Clearly if a competitor knows a business is for sale this is generally detrimental as they can use this in competitive situations with customers, they can poach employees and also go after strategic supplier relationships.

Family members - Often business owners do not share the fact they are for sale with family members. One reason is that a family member can potentially let the cat out of the bag (often inadvertently) with all of the above people.

There can also be a lot of fear and uncertainty with certain family members, which may not be helpful. Children also need to be treated with caution as they will often socialise with other children of companies in the above categories and inadvertently let slip the business is for sale.

Staying Confidential

There are 4 ways that we make sure that a business sale stays confidential:

1. Generic Teasers - We make all teasers that would be used for outreach anonymous with the specific company not identifiable. These teasers must be approved by the Seller to make sure there are no small clues someone who knew their business could pick up on. A good example is how long they have been in business or some feature or tagline that is specific to them. Another step is that a teaser will only be sent to the companies or groups of companies that the Seller specifically identifies as being 'safe'.

2. Signed NDAs - Any Buyers to whom we are going to supply the Confidential Information Memorandum (CIM) and reveal the company's name must sign a strict Non-Disclosure Agreement (NDA). This explicitly states that they are not allowed to share even the fact this business is for sale with anyone else. We have remarkably few problems with this happening once an NDA is signed.

3. Culture - The third way of keeping everything confidential is to create a culture where everyone understands how important this is. Within a good business M&A Advisory practice, this will mean everyone from the receptionist to the managing director will have had training around how important this is and ways of preventing any problems.

For example, it is essential that no one in the office tells their children about the businesses that the office has for sale. Children talk to other children in the community and one small comment at a social event can cause the fact the business is for sale to spread like wildfire.

4. Controlled Site Visits - Site visits can be challenging as staff may wonder who these people they don't recognise are. For this reason, we generally limit site visits if the staff that are not meant to know about the sale are present.

If we do need to go on-site, we normally try to go after hours and/or construct a cover story so as not to arouse suspicion. Often Buyers and Sellers will meet in person at the M&A Advisors office or a local hotel/restaurant or even at the Seller's house to avoid detection.

Confidentiality is critical in a business sale and is something that the Seller deserves as their ongoing business should not be impacted by the business sale process. With the proper training, policies, procedures and culture, 99% of the time any issues with confidentiality can be avoided.

Chapter 12 - Working with Advisors

Buying a business is one of the biggest challenges a person may undertake in their life next to getting married and having children. It may also be one of the most complex, yet most people who own businesses only do this once or maybe twice in their careers. Due to this, working with professionals that specialise in the business sale process can make the business sale journey a lot less stressful with a better outcome.

Buying a business is a team sport which needs a group of strong professionals to support clients during the process. The following are advisors that generally make up the team on the Sellers side:

Merger & Acquisition (M&A) Advisor – Sort of the quarterback that coordinates the process from beginning to end. We will structure the transaction, manage to post Heads of Terms process through closing, support the client's interests and keep everyone including the Buyer and Seller, together and calm when things get stressful and bring the champagne on closing day!

Business Lawyer – Their main role is to draft the legal contracts once due diligence is complete, the main document usually being the Share Purchase Agreement and about 15 other ancillary documents. They will also typically perform legal due diligence and may even be asked to advise on the Heads of Terms early in the process.

Personal Lawyer – These can be the same but are often different as the personal lawyer can advise the Buyer as an individual shareholder. This is common when more than one person owns the shares. They can also assist with any post-sale consultancy contracts, share schemes or employment.

Accountants – The Buyer generally first engages a specialist M&A accountant to assist with the due diligence process and business modelling. The M&A accountants are also generally needed throughout the process to answer accounting queries and assist the Buyer with personal tax matters. They will also review the SPA to make sure the numbers are correct and generally manage the closing account process.

Both parties will rely on the incumbent accountant who initially is responsible for producing historical accounts. They will generally be asked to produce management accounts up to the current period as well as closing accounts after the sale.

Personal Financial Planner – The Financial Planner can work with the Buyer to develop a comprehensive investment strategy for the Buyer and their family that maximises returns and minimises tax.

Tax Advisor – They will work with the accountant and wealth manager on any business or personal tax matters relating to the transaction.

Property Lawyer – If the business has freehold properties, usually a de-merger of the property out of the company being sold is executed, which requires specialist assistance.

Which Advisor?

There are many different advisors that will be happy to have the project work. The following are a few basic principles that will help a Seller choose the right one:

Education and Qualification - Experience and education are very important, the M&A process is very complex. It takes on average 4 months to buy a business once the Seller is engaged and there are many accounting, legal and functional challenges along the way.

Due to this, the advisor must be very knowledgeable to be able to guide the Buyer during the process. Ideally, the advisor will have the appropriate professional qualifications. But at the very least, they should have several years of experience and many transactions under their belt.

Reputable Firm With a Significant Track Record - Like with everything in the business world, a successful firm will have developed policies and practices over time to optimise the service they offer. Business sales is a team sport with many different players, so a larger firm will have a deep bench, so to speak. They will also have a management hierarchy the Buyer can access should issues arise.

Dedicated Advisor - Although the Buyer will want to work with an organisation as above, it is important that there is one point person that they trust that is the main point of contact. A business sale process is very involved and can take several months, so continuity is important.

What Role Does the M&A Advisor Play?

Negotiating Commercial Terms - We have discovered that the quickest way for people not to like each other is to talk about money and particularly the value of their business. Due to this, it is much more efficient for commercial discussions to be done through the advisor.

These kinds of transactions are very complex and this allows the advisor time to work with the Buyer and Seller on the offers, then taking time to explain thoroughly the offers to the Seller and then work with the Buyer and Seller on counter offers. This is done one-on-one so there is little emotion or need for defensiveness and allows a process to take place which is mostly about financial engineering.

Project Management - Once the Buyer and Seller have agreed on terms, there will be many weeks of due diligence, funding activities, legal, post-sale, planning, etc. It is the advisor's job to create and manage a plan for this, including regular meetings and updates with Buyer and Seller. At Transworld M&A we use our Dynamic M&A Transaction Management Program to make sure deals close as quickly as possible.

Managing Due Diligence - We will work with one of our accounting specialists who will analyse the results of due diligence and provide feedback and a report. This is essential as a specialist (almost always a chartered accountant) will know what they are looking for.

Business Modelling for Lending and Forward Cash Flow Planning - We will work with our accountant specialist who will prepare any necessary models. This requires a specialist who knows what the lenders are looking for and can help set the business up for proactive cash flow management.

Post-Sale Business Scale Up - We work with our finance and marketing professionals who specialise in Scale Up journey post-sale. Although this text is focused on actually acquiring the business, the post-sale journey and success of the business rely on proper systems and strategies. Our specialist can help you put in place the right systems, and assist with the implementation of sales and marketing strategies, as well as executive coaching.

Business Broker or Mergers and Acquisitions (M&A) Advisor?

Business brokers tend to work on smaller transactions, often on the high street. One way to look at it is that Business Brokers generally sit somewhere between property agents and M&A Advisors. Property agents are not trained to deal with an asset that is producing cash flow and all the ramifications that go with that so a business broker is required. However, business brokers are generally not trained or experienced in all the anomalies with funding, tax planning, complex equity structures, etc. that go with the larger transactions.

M&A Advisors can work on transactions up into the billions and with public companies so this is, on the face of it, a broad category. Generally, the M&A Advisors that work with smaller businesses are in a segment called Small to Medium Sized Enterprises (SME).

Generally, the more experienced, better trained and certified the advisor is, the more effective they will be as with most other things in the world of business. M&A Advisors tend to have more training and should have engaged in significant education as well as gained certifications as a demonstration. Many of them started off as brokers early in their careers, so also have more experience.

This is just a general guideline, who the Seller works with largely comes down to an individual preference for a specific firm or person.

Can a Buyer Buy a Business Without Help?

The answer to this question is yes, of course. As with all things in life, you could also service your own car, do your own plumbing, and file your own taxes. But does it really save any money? When you have a very complex transaction with many moving parts over four to six months, what are the chances the average person is going to engineer the best, multi-dimensional deal structure on the first go?

Also, the general statistic that is discussed is that 75% of transactions fall through before they even make the closing table. A further 50% don't deliver the value that was expected. Much of this is due to poor cultural fit and lots of mistakes during the Post Sale Process that alienate both parties from each other. A good M&A Advisor who has 1000's of hours of experience (and mistakes) can help a Buyer walk through this minefield greatly increasing the chances of closing and much faster...both of these save significant amounts of money for the Buyer.

The following are the challenges that you as a Buyer would need to overcome:

Pricing/Commercial - How do you know what a business is worth? Transactions are not just a number, they have many facets...how do you balance them all to get the right deal structure for a Seller that will survive until the closing table? Even one aspect missed could cost you £100Ks or a complete failure and starting again. Also, there is a direct cost for every day of delay in closing a deal. Just take the after-tax profit of the acquisition target and divide by 52 to calculate the weekly cost of inefficiency in the process to the Buyer (i.e. £520K after-tax profit would be £10K a week).

Negotiation - People that might otherwise like each other fall out and become offended when discussing money (think prenups, the couple would almost never discuss these themselves and still think the wedding was happening, they would let the lawyers do this). There is a process to mitigate this that has been developed over many years (and many mistakes). Obviously, an individual doing this for the first time has no access to this. Mistakes in this area can be very costly. Can you afford them?

Transactions are also complex with closing payments, deferred payments, earn-outs, stock rollover, penalty clauses, warranties, etc. Many things have to be balanced together. Do you want to take the time to understand all of this and are you willing to live with rookie mistakes? (Note: there is generally a lot of money involved, so even small mistakes are expensive).

Project Management - There are many things to do over many months including due diligence handling, funding, legal, post-sale planning, etc. All of these have to come together to get a transaction over the line. Do you want to have to learn what all of these are and if so, do you really want to have to manage all of them? It can become a full-time job for 6 months and distract you from other activities.

Deal Fatigue - This is a very real phenomenon, generally towards the last few weeks of a transaction (generally in the legal phase) which few people escape. It can cause significant emotional swings for both Buyer and Seller, as tempers fray and one small thing could cause one of them to call time on the entire process. A good M&A advisor will be aware of deal fatigue and be there to counsel both parties, keep everything calm and work through issues to avoid major blow-ups leading to deal failure.

A Friend To Take the Journey With You - A good M&A advisor is like a Sherpa guiding you up to the top of the mountain. They should be experienced in running the negotiation, due diligence, contracts, etc process guiding the process to avoid all the potential pitfalls. They are a confidant that will walk with you and share their experience and expertise every step of the way. They are someone to talk to that understands the detail. If you hit a problem even they cannot help with, they will have colleagues that can...so you will not walk alone. Buying a business can be very emotional, so this kind of support can be invaluable.

Chapter 13 - What to Expect

Post Sale

Once the deal is closed, there is a sense of relief more than anything. The last couple of weeks can be intense as all the details come together and everyone just needs a break. However, this is where the next phase begins as announcements need to be made to the staff, banking relationships changed, customers are informed, and a new management structure is potentially implemented, to name a few.

Telling the Staff -This can be one of the more nerve-racking steps in the process. There should be a good plan for what the messaging is going to be and a decision about whether the Buyer is going to be there. Often it is best to announce that an investor has become involved as the expectation is that the company will be growing. This puts everyone at ease as the leadership they are accustomed to is not leaving at least at that point. Key staff will often have bonuses related to the acquisition and usually, these should be discussed with them separately.

Transferring Bank Authority - The Buyer needs to take control of the bank and credit facilities, but this can take quite some time (sometimes months). Unfortunately, this step can generally not be taken until the day after closing (in case the deal does not close). Due to this, it is important to make a plan with the Seller to make sure that payments and bank transactions are continued until the transfer. Often this can be as easy as the Seller giving the Buyer their electronic banking login details in the interim.

Informing Customers - The process for this will vary from company to company and between different customers. The guiding principle here is to use common sense and not take any steps that might cause customers to seek to do business elsewhere. Again, the investor versus business sale angle can be used, the Seller can inform the customers personally or a general announcement can be sent out. Again, the guiding principle should be what will instil customer confidence.

A Modified Management Structure - This will generally be implemented in some form. It is important to get the buy-in from key people, document any changes and be clear on any new reporting requirements. The rule of thumb is to take this slowly to allow people to adjust and develop a positive attitude about the acquisition.

The Hand Over

Often the Seller will have an active role in the business during a transition period. The goals and plan for the transition period should be well documented during the post-sale planning phase in parallel with the due diligence process. The handover process can take many forms depending on the company but the goal should be continuity and the least disruption possible, particularly around customer service.

Many owners will take a more focused role after the handover, the most common being some business development responsibility for the major accounts they have relationships with. This allows the owner to stay involved and make a tangible contribution to the company as long as they are willing.

Generally, the transition period is planned to last for around 6 months. In practice, there is a certain momentum and it happens a lot faster. This is particularly the case if existing staff are taking over leadership roles. In that case, often the owner finds themselves sort of written out of the script and stepping back much quicker than the 6 month period.

Chapter 14 -

The 5 Steps to Scale Up Your Acquisition –

Paul Avins, The Grown Up Business Coach

For the last year, I've been working with Ken as part of my F12 Mastermind. So, I was very excited that he asked me to contribute a guest chapter to this new book.

In this chapter, I'm going to walk you through my proven 5-Step Scale-Up Framework. It's helped my coaching and mastermind clients add millions to the value of the companies they have acquired. It will also save you years of wasted time, energy and money if you apply what I'm about to cover in the next 5 steps.

So make sure you have a pen ready, or your phone handy to take notes as we have a lot to cover. Plus look out for the **FREE** resources I've listed at the end of the chapter.

Growing a business through acquisitions can be a powerful and lucrative strategy, but what happens when you've taken ownership? How do you start to identify and maximise growth opportunities?

Scaling up a business without a proven formula to follow will make it harder to create lasting value and freedom.

Without the right proven approach, you are using trial and error which is costly in both time and money. With no guarantee of success but a definite guarantee of stress!

Let's start with the end in mind.

S = Strategy and Sales

According to the Institute of Directors, over 80% of SME's in the UK have NO written down business plan. In my experience, this is why so many fail in less than 5 years. We don't want that to happen to you.

So, it's critical to start with a clear scale-up strategy that gets everybody on the same page. It also needs to drive sales growth.

Without a clear written down strategy for growth, every idea will seem like a good one. The key to a good strategy is it helps you know what to say "no" to as you grow so you stay focused.

Your Strategic Plan should cover the following 7 areas:

- The Vision and Values
- The Mission and Metrics
- The Dream Customer Clarity
- The Key Marketing Messages
- The Customer Profit Model
- The Team Dynamic Org Chart
- Your 12 Week MAP (Massive Action Plan)

The timeframe of your growth objectives will differ depending on if you're buying a business turning over £250K or £5m. But this framework with help you and your team stay on track. Set clear goals and use your strategy to navigate uncertain economic times.

Remember Sales happen when potential clients, get to know, like and trust you. Only then will they be open to transacting with you.

Add value in advance. Play the long game. Build relationship depth and create irresistible offers people feel crazy saying no to!

C = Customers and Cash

Customers are the lifeblood of the business you have acquired. You are going to want to divide them up into the following categories.

Then you can plan out how best to work with them, and market to them. I coach clients to divide customers into four categories.

A = High Profit, but Low Effort to support and maintain. These should be your dream customers, and we want more of them. These are the key ones to meet with. Reassure them they are in safe hands with you and build rapport.

B = High Profit, but also High Effort and cost to support. Worth sending them a video message or hosting a call for them to connect with. Often, they don't realise they are "high maintenance" so tell them. With good account management they can become "A" customers for you.

C = Low Profit and Low cost to support. These will be fine with a PR Release of e-mail update on the change of ownership. They offer great opportunities to upgrade in the future. Remember they will usually buy more from you if you educate them first about everything you offer.

D = Low Profit and high cost to support. High stress generators on your team! These are the ones you may want to visit to either re-negotiate terms or to release all together. Either outcome is a win for the business and will build trust with the team.

All the money and cash you need to fund expansion or pay back the owner is in the hands of your customers. The key is to get good at making them offers for products and services that would feel crazy to say not to!

Focus on ensuring customers get real results. Then they become raving fans who also refer new customers into the business.

A = Assets and Automation

The next most important area to look at now we own the business is the current assets. Both digital and physical.

This is why you need to do an Asset Audit in the first 90 days of ownership. To be honest if you can, do it in due diligence.

Here are my top categories to audit. You are looking to see what the company has but also where you can add/create new assets that add value.

People Assets - Organisation Chart / Position Contracts / Appraisal Process / Recruitment & Onboarding System

- **Product Assets** - Sales brochures / Quality Photos /
- **Marketing Assets** - CRM System / Clear Customer Journey / Client Testimonials / Videos / Sales Funnels
- **Brand Assets** - Brand Bible / Social Media Accounts / Endorsements / Books
- **Financial Assets** - Balance Sheet / Financial Forecasts / Budgeting tools / Scorecards / Dashboards
- **IP Assets** - Trademark Protections / Patents / Licensing Agreements

As you look to scale the businesses these assets become critical to building the balance sheet value. Remember that cash follows the creation of the right kind of asset. Map out a 90 day plan to create critical missing assets.

Documenting the current processes in the business is the next important step. There are some great software tools for this. Here is a link to a free 1hr Training on using systems to save 15hrs a week:

https://www.paulavins.com/airmanualwebinar

As AI starts to help us automate tasks, we need to look for opportunities to harness its power to save time and money.

L = Leadership and Leverage

You can't buy a business in the belief that you can leave it alone or that you can run it without any involvement from yourself.

That is not the case in my experience. There is always a level of involvement and direction from the business owner or investor.

We often refer to it as "Leaders Energy". Without it team members often leave, customers stop buying and profits start falling.

Harnessing the power of other people's talents and energy is one of the best forms of Leverage in a business. Especially if you want to scale up. To do this you need to become a better Leader.

Here are 6 success traits I've seen my top clients exhibit post-acquisition with their new team.

Great Listening skills that build deep trust in others

Engages and energises others with their vibrant vision

Hold themselves and others accountable

Delivers for the team, customers and shareholders

Empowers people to maximise their contributions

Is Real and Raw understanding they will make mistakes

Leverage money is another key leverage tool. These options to fund your growth may include bank loans, asset finance, other lines of credit. The key here is never to use this money to solve cash flow problems. Instead only to use it to create marketing assets like videos or sales funnels. Campaigns to drive traffic or systems and technologies that will save you time.

The final option is to use it to recruit the talent you need to grow to the next level. Remember it's not about working harder as a Leader it's about harnessing the power of Leverage.

E = Execution Excellence and Exit Planning

As I have said for years "you get paid on what you get...Done!' after all talk is cheap execution is the real success skill of entrepreneurs.

Included is a graphic that many of our clients find very helpful to make sure they stay in the investor role. This is especially important after an acquisition.

The danger is having taken the previous owner out of the business you find yourself getting pulled into daily operations. While you may have to do this short term, its critical to have a clear Growth MAP (Massive Action Plan) to follow.

This will help you to get more done in 12 weeks than most people get done in 12 months! After all, the power of focus is following one course until successful.

So, make sure you start with the end in mind. Where you want to be in 3/5 years. Work backwards and create that 12/18 month Mission with clear metrics attached.

As any good coaching session always ends with some questions:

So, what did you get more value from in the framework I shared?

What actions are you going to take in the next 72 hours?

Who can you share these with to hold you accountable?

What Community do you need to be around to get you fired up and ready to grow? (Ok that one was a bit of a leading question :-))

Remember - Simple scales and complex fails!

Let's connect on LinkedIn where I share daily content. My goal is to help you build a Grown Up Business you can sell for Millions.

Connect with Paul on LinkedIn - www.linkedin.com/in/paulavins

Who is Paul Avins and why do so many Entrepreneurs and Investors Trust him?

As CEO of Paul Avins Enterprises he helps ambitious entrepreneurs build scalable businesses.

He coaches and mentors his clients to achieve seven figures in sales, profits and real shareholder exit value. (Over £27m of exits in 2022 alone!)

With his skilled team he runs 2 day live events, 6 and 12 month Masterminds and his 4 day Grown Up Business Retreat.

Paul is an award-winning business coach with over 20 years experience. He is the author of 5 business books and appears on Podcasts all over the world to share his insights and ideas.

Paul has coached over 550 UK companies through this Grown Up Business growth system. If there is a clear scale-up blueprint for success, Paul has it!

Access Paul's FREE Scale Up Growth resources below:

To download the eBook - 7Steps to 7Figures visit:
www.7Figurebook.paulavins.com

To watch Paul's Free Scale Up Masterclass at
www.scaleupmasterclass.co.uk

Download Paul's 67 Business Growth Tips Book

https://www.paulavins.com/67-growth-tips

Learn about Europe's No1 Business Retreat for Entrepreneurs

https://www.grownupbusinessretreat.com

Chapter 15 - Basic Business Buyer Education

On a daily basis, the M&A sector, which includes Buyers looking for acquisitions, is focused on the activities of acquiring a business as if this were some kind of end in itself. However, often the day eventually comes when an acquisition actually happens and now it is time to run the business...as an Owner.

In this chapter, we wanted to outline several skills we think are important for the new Owner of the business should have. Much of this can be learned through online courses, books, seminars and/or with specialised consultants with a little bit of effort. But the key is that whatever skills you don't have will need to be learned somewhere, so education will be essential. Even if you are employing people in these areas, you will want to understand them well enough to 'Direct & Lead' and make intelligent decisions on strategy and resource allocation.

Basic Accounting - It is critical as a business owner to be able to understand Profit/Loss, Balance Sheet and how they relate to cash flow. These are the fundamental tools for managing, valuing and doing tax planning. Without a working knowledge of these reports, an owner finds himself at the mercy of outside advisors for decision making, which rarely works well.

Cash Flow Management - Most businesses that go out of business have as a root cause that the directors are not able to manage cash flow effectively. The general advice is that all businesses should have at least 12 months of forward cash flow planning. This generally is not created by the owner but by the finance director or someone in that role. But understanding it and managing it is critical.

Business Planning - Similar to cash flow planning, it is important to have a plan for how the business is going to grow and what resources are needed. This will include sales projections, increases in staff, marketing, stock, etc. This becomes the blueprint for how the business will grow.

Management and Recruiting - Team building and team management are the essence of most businesses, as businesses are full of people. Recruiting and team building are skills that can be learned. Our experience is that few people are born with these skills, and many don't like these areas as they don't know what to do and think they should somehow have these skills naturally. But they are actually mostly learned skills with many techniques, processes and systems that can and should be studied.

Marketing 101 - Lead generation and brand awareness are keys to most businesses. Many people fancy themselves as marketers, but that only goes so far. Things are moving so fast that what worked one day may be old news the next. The key is to plug into a mastermind group or marketing guru that is constantly staying up to date. As a director, it is also key to understand all of the different marketing opportunities and their expected result to know where to allocate time and money for the biggest return. However, as always, consistency is key in marketing and the right resources need to be allocated to enable this consistency.

Business Processes - Understanding and optimising processes is key in almost every business. Good processes mean better and quicker customer service, better margins and happier customers and employees. There are very good consultants in the community who specialise in this very aspect and can come into the business and work with the directors on a regular basis to continuously optimise and document business processes.

Running a Board and Non-Exec Team - This is a very different skill set than being part of the executive and the Managing Director who runs the day-to-day business. The board will only sit periodically but will provide vital strategy and governance to the business. Many inexperienced owners have benefited from hiring an experienced, non-exec Chairman to run the board for them. This is a great way to get experience in the business and take some stress off a new owner and have someone to call.

Personal Development - This aspect is much more important than many people understand as they see it as a nice to have when they get time, maybe like going to the gym. It turns out that one of the biggest limiting factors of a business being successful is the mindset of the owner so this area may actually be one of the first to invest in. Removing the blocks in your own mind and creating a visionary mindset is something most people can do with help and good coaching. Paul Avins, who has written a chapter in this book, is one of the leading experts in the UK for business and personal scaling up.

There are obviously many more areas we could cover but it might be overwhelming. We feel this list is doable in a few months with the right plan and effort. Ironically, doing the last one first (personal development coaching) may help a new Buyer get in the right mindset and create this plan where they may have been struggling with limiting beliefs, time management issues or lack of motivation. Each new business owner is different, but the basics are generally the same and knowledge really is power.

Chapter 16 - Potential Challenges During the Process

This chapter covers the situations we have learned through hard experiences delay or kill transactions completely. Business sale transactions are time-consuming, expensive and completing them is important (as the owner often has an appointment with the beach!). So making an effort to understand and avoid or mitigate these issues early on can make all the difference.

Poor Books and Records

Poor books and records is one of the main reasons that the due diligence phase ends up with the transaction not continuing. At a high level, the Buyer is buying future cash flow and they need to be able to rely on all the different elements that make up that cash flow.

We normally work with 3 years of filed accounts, which the accountant would have prepared, and we expect them to be accurate. We then work with management accounts out of the Seller's accounting systems since the last filed accounts date (fiscal year). This allows the Buyer to see that the business is on track during the most recent months. So if this basic reporting is not available, it makes it very difficult for a Buyer to get comfortable and almost impossible to get commercial lending.

Beyond that, specific areas that tend to cause problems are debtor books, stock and work in progress. Debtor books which are inaccurate (i.e. don't reflect who owes the company money) have a knock-on effect on the P&L and Balance sheet (i.e. if a debtor isn't real, the sale didn't really happen). Also, if many debtors are over 90 days, questions arise as to whether the sales related to them were real.

Also, the stock must be accurate, as this may be one of the biggest items on the balance sheet. An incorrect stock figure impacts the Cost of Sale figure on the P&L which then can have a direct effect on EBITDA, which then in turn has an impact on the valuation. The same goes for the Work in Progress figure, anomalies translate directly to EBITDA and valuation in most cases.

The bottom line is that if it is discovered that the books are records can not be relied on, usually it is time to consider withdrawing from the transaction. An alternative is to encourage the Seller to engage an M&A accountant to reconstruct the books and take a view on whether these new reports are a more accurate reflection of past performance and indicate what future performance will be. Some businesses are really worth the effort, sort of wiping mud off diamonds!

Declining Financial Results

This issue occurs when the Buyer engaged in the transaction and valued the business with financial results from a previous period and may even have had up-to-date management accounts when the Heads of Terms were signed. However, over the several months that the due diligence/funding phase has run, the financial results have declined. This is obviously concerning for a Buyer as they are buying future cash flow which will often be determined by the run rate of the business at closing. If the results have declined, they may assume that this is the new run rate and therefore the business should be revalued. Needless to say, not welcome news to the Seller!

In this situation, the reason for the decline needs to be determined. If it is a one-off and temporary, there are measures that can be taken to keep the deal on track, but sharing the risk will be inevitable. If the downturn is deemed to be permanent, then the transaction may need to be renegotiated or terminated.

Lack of Cash at Closing

Lack of cash at closing can occur for several reasons. All of these are problematic as they can result in the Seller not getting their entire closing payment, the business not having enough cash to run, long-term debt not being paid off, etc. The main reason this arises is that the debtors have not paid at their normal rate which could be a fluke or because sales are down just before closing or the commercial lending is less than expected.

Often the teams are surprised when this happens at the last minute. To mitigate this, very careful cash flow planning should be done at least a month before closing and monitored very, very closely until the day of closing. Contingent plans should also be put in place if there is any chance an issue could arise.

Lawyer Issues

The process of working through an M&A transaction is much more like a wedding where two parties are coming together for the same mutually beneficial event, with a natural tension between both families and some pre-nuptials. The problem is that most lawyers are trained and geared toward managing a divorce and do not understand that an adversarial approach in an M&A transaction may kill what was actually a good deal for both people.

A good M&A lawyer will understand this and hold ground on important points but always have the bigger picture and respectful relationship that needs to exist between Buyer and Seller in mind. Due to this, it is very important to choose a lawyer with significant M&A experience and avoid lawyers that are mainly property oriented, for example.

The other issue we find with lawyers is that they tend to take on too much work and if your transaction is a small one and they have no 3rd party connection, your project may get pushed to a lower priority. Due to this, it is often helpful to choose a lawyer that regularly does work for the M&A Advisor or has some other connection to someone you know where performance on your transaction will have a good or bad wider impact on that relationship.

Accountant Issues

Accountants are vital team members during an M&A transaction. The Seller's accountant will need to produce historical reports as well as assist with future projects and validate the commercial framework and advise on tax issues. The first issue arises when the accountant is very slow to produce these reports and the project team is left waiting in limbo until they do. This is a difficult problem to solve and up to the Seller to put pressure on them to meet deadlines or consider hiring an outside M&A accountant to help with the transaction.

The other issue with accountants is that they often have very little training and exposure to key aspects of an M&A transaction. The first is that they do not really deal in 'risk'. For example, few people would ask their accountant which stock to buy on the stock market, this is intuitive. Yet risk runs through the M&A paradigm, driving everything from business valuations to payment terms and interest rates.

They also generally don't view the world through the personal situation of their clients (i.e. that the client needs to retire for personal reasons and it is not just about financial calculations). Most accountants also have little formal training in business valuation which is a different skill set than traditional accounting as it is forward looking, unlike most accounting which is about looking backwards.

Because of this, they will often be very negative on M&A transactions as they see their client losing a cash flow they have been enjoying for years and from their lense not understanding why they would give that up for what they consider to be a low sale price. However, our experience is that most accountants have their clients' best interests in mind and their opinion is important and worth considering but it should also be taken with a grain of salt for the reasons above.

The best approach for the Buyer is to get the accountant involved very early in the process. The M&A Advisor should be able to build rapport with them and invite them into the core team to they feel part of the transaction and can start to understand all aspects of it. Although they act for the Seller, they will be key in all the discussions around numbers and so having a good relationship with them is critical.

Choosing the Wrong M&A Advisor

The Buy Side M&A Advisor will generally manage the process from beginning to end, so if they are weak in any one or multiple areas, it can significantly compromise the process. This starts off with the ability to build rapport with the Seller and assist with structuring the transaction right through to managing due diligence and then the contracts phase.

They should also act as a sounding board for the Buyer to help them through difficult patches. They need to be savvy enough to help navigate the many twists and turns in the process otherwise the Buyer may be on their own or at the mercy of friends and family who have an opinion but generally little experience. So choosing the right Advisor, to begin with, is probably one of the most important decisions in the process to maximise the chances of getting to the closing table in a timely manner.

Dishonesty

The Seller is going to receive what could be £MMs of pounds for their business and rely on the future cash flows generated by the customer base and serviced by the employees and processes of the business to make any deferred payments as well as maintain their legacy. They will usually need to have total confidence in the Buyer and their integrity in order to conclude a transaction.

If they feel that the Buyer or someone working on the Buyer's team is being dishonest, this confidence can evaporate as well as their willingness to do the transaction. Our advice is to be honest in everything, as it builds trust. Also, to have the idea that over many months everything will be found out anyway, so there is no use being dishonest and better to deal with the truth. People respect each other that way and trust and respect are what get deals over the line.

Not Building Trust with the Buyer and Seller

This is related to the above point about dishonesty. Generally, the Seller is going to take many things on faith to gain the confidence necessary to be willing to relinquish control of their business to the Buyer. He will need to build trust in the Buyer's business acumen, values, business plan and resources to reach this level of confidence.

We always say that trust is what closes deals as there are always 2 or 3 things that come at the end that require both parties to compromise and take leaps of faith...the amount of trust that has been built during the process is directly related to how willing they will be to do this.

Landlord and Premise Lease Issues

Many businesses have premises that are required for them to operate, which are rented or leased. When a business is sold, many of these leases have conditions about changes in ownership and or personal guarantees that need to be transferred. Often, the leases have to be renegotiated with the landlord's legal council. The issue is that this whole process can be slow, tedious and time-consuming.

Usually, it is what it is and needs to be done if the Buyer wants to stay on the same premises. But having these negotiations is often left late in the process and ends up delaying the whole business sale. So the advice we give is to consider this a critical path item and to start this stream of work early knowing it could go very slowly, especially if the landlord is an institution in our experience.

Partnership Issues

Many businesses are owned by more than one person. However, often one person has a significant majority so is used to calling the shots. This majority shareholder is usually the one that initiates the business sale and is most involved in the process. Occasionally, when a significant amount of work has been done one of the minority shareholders decides that they are not in favour of the sale for some reason.

Most shareholder agreements have drag-along/tag along provisions which would mean, in theory, they can be forced to go along with the transaction but this can be costly and time-consuming. Therefore, it is usually prudent to make sure all of the shareholders are on board with the business sale before the process starts or be prepared early to deal with any legal action to force the transaction through if necessary.

Not Really Ready to Sell

In an earlier chapter, we discussed the 'switch' that needs to go off inside of a Seller, letting them know it is time to move on. This is just an analogy but, it demonstrates the idea that the Seller has to have some level of really wanting to sell their business.

If they are just lukewarm, they are unlikely to make the compromises necessary and put up with the multi-month headache that is generally the business sale process. As the process itself is such an investment for both Buyer and Seller, it is important that the Seller be sure early on that this is something they want to do.

Unreasonable Financial Expectations

The Seller has a right to want whatever they want for their business, no one should judge that as it is their asset. However, this may be more than is reasonably possible for any Buyer and also any lending institution. If the Seller's expectations are above what will work from a valuation, cash flow and lending perspective, the transaction will almost certainly fail when this is discovered. Again, as there is so much investment in a business sale transaction by both the Buyer and Seller, it is very important to evaluate this as early as possible.

Lack of Timely Follow-Up

Business sale transactions take a lot of focus from both Buyer and Seller who are often paying outside professionals to be part of the process. There is also just a natural pace and a certain energy level everyone devotes to it with an expectation of completing it in a reasonable time period.

If one side is very slow on responses, it can greatly affect the costs on the other side as well as focus. At some point, the other side may just give up and they will not see the transaction ever completed and move to another Buyer or Seller, they think they can get a result with. However, business sales should not be a pressure cooker as they go on for many months and people would become exhausted. They should, however, move at a reasonable pace with each side responding in a timely manner to keep the process going.

Bank Issues

There are many bank issues that can hold up a transaction. These can be a transfer of any loans with the change of ownership, the Buyer's lender nitpicking and taking forever to approve the lend for the transaction, releasing the mortgage on properties, the bank approving the transfer of credit lines and invoice financing, liens being removed from the company at Companies House (we have seen debt that was paid decades ago still not cleared in the public record), etc. These are all issues that have to be dealt with for a transaction to complete. The mitigation is to identify them early and start the process, knowing the speed of the bank is a limiting factor.

Government Issues

There are many issues I am grouping into a category called 'government' that can stall or stop a transaction. Everything from business licensing issues, personal licensing requirements, zoning and permits. But also outstanding legal issues and fines, back taxes, unresolved government court cases and investigations, etc. As always, mitigation is done by identifying these early and assessing the likelihood of resolution before too much cost is incurred in the process. If any of these items are left unresolved, there is also the possibility for a Seller to give warranties that if there is any kind of financial impact in the future, they will be covering the cost, usually as an offset to deferred payments.

Funding

No list of pitfalls would be complete without mentioning how many issues the attempt for the Buyer to secure funding can cause. The commercial lenders can be very tedious in their requests, demand audits, take illogical positions...and then disappear for long periods. Unfortunately, commercial lending is necessary for most business sale transactions so working through this is necessary. Our advice is for the Buyer to engage a specialist lending agent to assist in this process and stress test the lending as early as possible to make sure the transaction is viable.

Chapter 17 - Next Steps

Buying a business may be one of the biggest things you do in your lifetime, next to getting married and having children. It often ushers you into a whole new life, one you probably deserve for all the hard work put into getting to the closing table.

You should look to get the most out of the process and most often engaging a professional who has the experience and training as a Buy Side M&A Advisor can make a big difference. I wrote this book as I want to be that person (with my team, of course) for a number of people who read this. We can help with:

- Increase the chances of getting to the closing table.

- Accelerate the process which means getting profit in the Buyer's hands sooner

- Manage a process which allows people to sleep at night knowing everything is in hand

I feel it is our vocation to help people who want to buy and also those who want to sell get to a great conclusion as it is life-changing for both.

If you have found a business you would like to buy, we would love to help get you get it to the closing table.

Please feel free to contact me at:

Transworld M&A Advisors UK LSW

KGorman@transworldukmanda.co.uk

Whatever direction you go in, we wish you well on your M&A journey!